RAVE AMERICA

RAVE AMERICA
New School Dancescapes

Mireille Silcott

ECW PRESS

The publication of *Rave America* has been generously supported by the Canada Council, the Ontario Arts Council, and the Government of Canada through the Book Publishing Industry Development Program.

CANADIAN CATALOGUING IN PUBLICATION DATA

Silcott, Mireille, 1973-

Rave America: new school dancescapes

ISBN 1-55022-383-6

1. Techno music – Social aspects.
2. Rave culture.
I. Title.

ML.3540.S582   1999   781.64   C99-931994-9

Cover design by Benno Russell.
Interior design by Yolande Martel.

Printed by AGMV l'Imprimeur, Cap-Saint-Ignace, Quebec.

Distributed in Canada by General Distribution Services, 325 Humber College Blvd., Etobicoke, Ontario M9W 7C3.

Distributed in the United States by LPC Group, 1436 West Randolph Street, Chicago, Illinois, 60607. U.S.A.

Distributed in Europe by Turnaround Publisher Services Unit 3, Olympia Trading Estate, Coburg Road, Wood Green, London N2Z 6TZ.

Published by ECW Press, 2120 Queen Street East, Suite 200, Toronto, Ontario M4E 1E2.

www.ecw.ca/press

PRINTED AND BOUND IN CANADA

To my family, Mike, and Alana

Acknowledgments

This book would not have been possible without the years of preliminary research I was able to do in my former position as music editor of the Montreal *Mirror*. Thank-yous go to the *Mirror*'s senior editors, Alistair Sutherland and Annarosa Sabbadini, and I'm grateful for the encouragement of editors Chris Yurkiw and Matthew Hays as well. Thanks also to Streetsound's Chris Torella for the initial training he gave me on the ins and outs of writing about dance music when I was just a wee pup.

It would also have been impossible for me to write this book without the hands-on education I was given by the DJs, flyer designers, zine publishers, promoters, and club kids who have been both my friends and major sources of raging arguments (breakbeats vs straight beats! knobs vs cross faders! etc., etc.) over the past dozen years: Benno Russell, Gavin McInnes, Luc Raymond, Christian Pronovost, Tiga Sontag, Double A & Twist, Justin Dallagret, Nenad Andrasic, Stacey Langbein, and everybody in the Legendary House of Stitch Bitch. Thanks also to Chris Farley for being the first house DJ I ever heard and to Spike-E for first teaching me about the politics of ecstasy.

I am greatly indebted to Push in London for bearing with me, and to all the people back in North America who gave me hours of assistance and kindly opened up their contact books and clipping/flyer collections for me: Jason Joyal @ Shock, Kiki Dranias @ Channel, Wade Hampton, Woody McBride, Malachy O'Brien, Kerry Jaggers, Kurt Eckes, Jackie McLure, Tony Humphries and Chris @ Yellow Orange, José Torrealba and Ian, Sunshine Jones, Dianna Jacobs, Garth Wynne-Jones, Markie Mark Rowley, Jenö, Bevin O'Neil, John Marsa, Stace Bass, Beverly May, Kimball Collins, Welcome, Marco and Mauro Lavilla, Billy Caroll, Gavin Bryan @ Industry, AK1200, Robert Vezina @ the BBCM, and Patrick Dream. Double thanks to Junior

Vasquez for giving me a tape recorder when mine broke in New York, to
Dantech for supplying me with batteries and blank cassettes when my "technology" went bonkers in the middle of Nowhere, Wisconsin, and to all the
people who kindly drove me around Orlando, where walking is never an
option. Thanks also to Dawn for putting me up in Toronto, to Moonbeam
Jones for the weird vegan food in San Francisco, and to Keoki and Steven
Cohen @ Moonshine in Los Angeles for allowing me the ridiculous experience of conducting an interview in a stretch limo accompanied by a leather-
clad dog.

A few of the quotes in this book are taken from interviews conducted for
the Montreal *Mirror* or for the Much Music and Musique Plus TV stations
between the years 1994 and 1997. Particular thanks go to Frankie Knuckles,
Derrick May, Juan Atkins, Liam Howlett, and Cajmere for providing extra-
long and extrasuper interviews in 1996. But most of the interviews for this
book were granted to me by generous people with nothing much to gain
except a chance to reminisce about faces and places they never get to talk
about anymore. Many, many thanks to Tommie Sunshine. Thanks also to
Gaylen Abbot, Acid Boy Todd P, DJ Anabolic Frolic, John Angus, Alex @
Tribe, Steven Baird, Ashley @ Better Days Promotions, Pete Avila, DJ Buc,
Don Burns, Alan Brown, Andrew C., Dave Canalte, Robbie Clark @ Under-
ground Records, Alex Clive, DJ Daisy, DJ Dominik, Anthony Donnely, Dose,
DJ D-Xtreme, John E, MC E-by-Gum, Craig @ MW Raves, Chris Hand, Robbie
Hardkiss, Scott Hardkiss, Danny Henry, John Howard, Cody Hudson, Andy
Hugues, Tom Hunter, DJ Icey, Tommy Illfingaz, Joe in Dallas, Jungle PHD,
Steven Keller, Kid Batchelor, Ryan Kruger, Terrence Leung, Steven Levy
@ Moonshine, Rob Lisi @ Syrous/Renegades, DJ Marcus, Matt & Brad @
Massive, Mike & Charlie, Mike @ Salvation, Chad Mindrive, Mr. Bill, Mr. C
@ The End, Mystical Influence, Nick @ Global UK, Nick Nice @ Nice
Musique, Martin O'Brien, Mark Oliver, Peter Primiani @ 83 West, Andrew
Rawnsley @ *XLR8R*, Rod Roderick, Art Roger, Rich Rosario, DJ Ruffneck,
James St. Bass, Ira Sandler @ 1015, DJ Sandy, DJs Slip n' Slide, DJ Spice, DJ
Spinz, Sniper, Cliff T, Eli Tobias, MC Trigger, Tyler @ Revolutions, Mike
Vance, and Jason Walker. Sincere apologies to anyone I may have forgotten.

I am extremely grateful to Will Straw for his constant support and help,
to Robert Lecker and Holly Potter at ECW for being the most patient people
on earth, and to Alana Klein for her tireless dedication, her tenacity, and her
ears of steel. I have deep gratitude for my family and for Mike Kronish —
they provided moral support and continually slipped long-distance "I Luv
Yous" under the proverbial door.

Contents

Preamble

When I first started researching this book, in January of 1997, there were no books on the market about the history of American house music in the 1970s and 1980s written from a North American perspective, but I figured that by the time this book was finished, there would be. So I decided to write a book about 1990s American rave culture — a later and much different school of America's nightworld — thinking that my little book could serve as a neat adjunct to the work of whoever was going to write about the stuff that came before.

It is now May of 1999, and that book on the history of house music has still not been published. Some of the more pertinent bits of house music's early history are included in chapter 1 of this book. However, if you would like to know more about the seventies and eighties clubs and studios of New York, Chicago, Detroit — the main hives of early house — I'd suggest you look at some recent books by British authors: most notably, Simon Reynolds's *Energy Flash*, a veritable encyclopedia of British rave culture that devotes a couple of extensive chapters to American house developments (the US edition of this book is called *Generation Ecstasy*).

I really don't wish to imply that "classic" American house was or is better or more important than American rave. Rather, I want to stress that this is a book about a *second* wave — hence the subtitle *New School Dancescapes* — a book mainly about what happened after American house music was imported to Britain, mixed with the drug ecstasy creating a cultural explosion, and then returned to American turf looking very different from the way it did when it left.

Rave was, for the most part, brought to North America by expat Britons or people who had traveled to Europe and wanted to replicate what they had seen there. And, transplanted in North America, it underwent some initial growing pains. But even so, usually within months of landing on a new patch of North American soil, the culture began morphing into shapes organic to its new location. Chapters 2 to 5 of this book look at some of the cities in which North American rave took on very distinct regional flavors. Chapter 6 deals with a culture comparable to rave, a culture of completely North American origin — the all-night dance parties of the gay circuit, what some have called "gay raves."

Although the chapters are arranged in a loosely chronological order, charting where North American raves happened first and showing how they gained momentum in smaller centers throughout the nineties, I hope that you will start by reading the chapter that interests you most. This book is by no means an all-inclusive history; it's just a collection of some of the most vibrant, nutty, roller-coaster-ish and all-out original party scenes of North America's last decade.

PROLOGUE
A Midwest Raver Goes to Storm Rave — A First-Person Account

"I have kept a journal all my life. Everything is written down in psychotic detail," says Tommie Sunshine. "So this oral history I'm about to tell you, well, it's all true. I swear it's all true.

"My friends and I had a ritual. We were traveling ravers. That's to say, every Friday it was pack your bags, drive wherever the party was, it didn't matter how far — our car was our ticket to freedom. Half the time, we didn't have anyone to stay with at our final destination. We would get into whatever city it was, buy our tickets at a record store, get our map to the party, drive to the party site, park, and get some sleep in the car. We would set the alarms on our watches — this was before pagers and cell phones were big. We'd get up, go to a Denny's and change, get into our full rave gear, and then the fun started. We would meet as many people as we could at the rave, and nine times out of ten we would meet someone who would let us stay at their house, because at that point in the game, like, we all trusted each other. We were ravers. This was 1992.

"It was in December of that year that I went to a New York Storm Rave. December 12, 1992. So help me God, I will remember that date forever! We rented a van: this girl Catherine and Kurt Eckes from Milwaukee's [party-promotions outfit] Drop Bass Network, Tony Kaminsky, who threw parties as Sense Productions in Chicago, and myself, Tommy Sunshine, twenty-one years old, 'celebrity raver' from the suburbs of Chicago, the kid every raver in the Midwest knows.

"So we set forth on this fourteen-hour drive to Brooklyn from Chicago. It's Friday night, midnight, and DJ Bad Boy Bill is on the radio. In Ohio, we hook up with another van, loaded with people from Cincinnati. We met at an exit. I am talking a two-van caravan from the Midwest to New York for a party, because we had read [Storm rave organizer] Heather Heart's magazine *Under One Sky* and we had to know what this Storm thing was all about. We didn't know it then, but the party we were going to was to be the last Storm Rave ever.

"In some stroke of insanity, I had brought my boom box with me on this trip, and I secretly recorded all of us talking in the car for most the ride. If you heard these tapes now, you would not believe them — all we talked about the whole time was our favorite DJ's and 'who did the most E, nitrous balloons, acid last weekend.' We were so naïve. Darkness had not hit the Midwest rave scene yet, it was still all pigtails, smiles, and glitter — all happy stuff, right? And so when we got to the Storm site, we were shocked.

"I had never seen anything like what I saw that night: seven thousand people in a horse stable, on Staten Island, in the mud. We were up to our ankles in mud. But that's not what shocked me. It was the people. Everybody seemed *hard* and *dark* and almost *mean*. Like, the girls were wearing baseball caps, with fucking black hoodies up over them — you couldn't even fucking tell they were chicks . . . all slam dancing to [DJs] Jimmy Crash, Adam X, Frankie Bones, Lenny Dee, Keoki, and special guest from LA Sandra Collins.

"So here I am at this scary Storm Rave, wearing my stupid Midwest-rave-kid-happy-suit, looking around, and seeing pure insanity. Not only am I up for like a day with no sleep, but I had also decided it would be a fun idea to 'candy flip' — do a hit of E and a hit of acid — at Storm Rave. Not a very good idea under any circumstances, especially these. I remember standing around with some of the promoters . . . one's name was Eddie Van Raven and the other was Dennis the Menace. Dennis asks us if we wanted to get high. Yes we did! So the [pipe] bowl goes 'round. I'm thinking, 'Wow, I've never smoked pot that tasted like burning *plastic* before.' Bowl goes 'round again. I'm thinking, 'Something is really weird about this pot,' so I go, 'Excuse me, Dennis the Menace, but what *kind* of pot is this?' 'It's dust,' he says. So I'm on E, acid, no sleep, and now a quarter bowl of angel dust with coke sprinkled on top. . . .

"And suddenly the music hits me — the drugs, the music, the sleeplessness, *pang*! It's Lenny Dee; he's just gotten on the decks. There was a twenty-five-foot chain-link fence between the crowd and the DJ booth. The sound system was so huge and powerful that if they hadn't set the crowd about thirty feet back from the speakers our eardrums would have exploded. For real. Imagine the biggest sound system you have ever seen at a party or a concert. Well, here there is one to the left of the DJ booth and one to the right.

"And Lenny Dee? He's playing records, thrashing around like he's in a fucking punk band. When he's done with his records he's holding them up over his head, like, 'I am the vinyl messiah!' The crowd cheers, and then Lenny smashes the record on the wall behind him. And I'm just trying to make any sense out of what's going on. Like if I *hadn't* been on any of these drugs it would have been fucking insane, but add insult to injury, like, I'm at brain-Disneyland at this point . . . I can't even look at it like it's *real* anymore, because it's too over the top. There are kids climbing all the way up the fence — twenty-five feet high, hanging onto the fence, screaming at Lenny Dee, 'Faster! *Faster!!!!*' and he's playing tracks that are 180 [BPMs]! All this German extreme techno! And they want more? These New York maniacs want if *faster*?!

"Then [DJ] Frankie Bones gets on. He was obviously the Pope of Brooklyn. Frankie fucking Bones, with his leather jacket and his crazy Brooklyn accent. He puts a record on a turntable and yells into the mike: 'This is the first time I have ever played this song! This song is *about* Storm Rave, this song is *for* Storm Rave, this is "Show 'Em We Can Do This!"' If you listen to that record now, it sounds like shit, but at the time it had so much relevance. It had a Public Enemy sample — 'show 'em we can do this, show 'em we can do this' — looped over and over, and, after a couple of minutes, you want to fucking *show them we can do this*! Whatever the hell 'this' is.

"So, the seven thousand kids are reading special messages into this track. After all, Frankie told them it was *made* for them. And the place has become a fucking three-ring circus! Now there are kids climbing up the fence and *jumping off* the fence, into the crowd, like mosh pit. There are people getting passed around the crowd. There are, at this point, drugs being done in purely plain view: kids leaning up against a fence, tying up their arms, and shooting fucking Ecstasy. Shooting E! And at that point, I was split in two: I was enjoying it all, but I started feeling like I was *somewhere bad*. I knew that this might be the wrong fork in the road for rave, like maybe this wasn't the best route for us.

"I don't think I could talk for three weeks after I came home. I was shell-shocked. That night showed me how far you could take people through the combination of music and drugs. Right to the extremes, that's what rave is for — Storm rave, a kiddie-candy rave, any rave. You are alive! Alive! Alive! Us ravers, we were just a buncha dumb American kids. We weren't historicizing; nothing really mattered to us except for the present. We had no fear of our future, and our past was irrelevant. All we wanted was what we had. That distilled thing. In some instances, positive, in others, negative. But, whatever, the feeling was so extreme you just knew you had to go with it. Because it wouldn't last forever. Almost by definition, it couldn't. We may have been dumb kids, but we all knew that."

1 MUSICAL ROOTS AND REINVENTION
From the Disco to Storm Rave

1970–1977: New York City Disco

In the 1970s, when New York clubland was in full disco swing, two clubbers on the underground circuit became good friends — a man named Laurence Philpot, who had renamed himself Larry Levan when he started clubbing because it "sounded better," and a Brooklyn kid named Frankie Knuckles, born Frances Nicholls. Knuckles was the "calm one." Levan was the "crazy one." As teens in the early 1970s, the duo — both gay, both Black — had worked as "vibesmen" at a disco called the Gallery. Their responsibilities included spiking the punch with LSD and, occasionally, injecting it into the free fruit the Gallery provided for the replenishment of tired dancers.

Seventies-era discos like the Gallery were the product of a euphoric time: America was no longer at war in Korea or Vietnam. The sexual revolution was manifesting itself. Gay liberation was pushing out of the closet. Urban integration was underway. And economic promise permeated the American air. The mainstreaming of recreational drugs such as LSD and marijuana had occurred in the late sixties. In the seventies, a guiltless pharmacopoeia — including cocaine, speed, sexy downers like Quaaludes, "psychedelic-amphetamines" like MDA and MDMA, and mindbenders like PCP (angel dust) — poured into the club scene. The result was an environment that was both keenly self-aware and open to anything.

The Gallery was part-owned by a young DJ named Nicky Siano. Nicky Siano took playing records seriously. In his pre-Gallery days, he used to sit around his mom's house trying to cleanly splice and mix two records into each other. Once Siano had his own club, he installed not two, but three turntables in his DJ booth so that he could insert effects into his record mixes — like a charging train, or an airplane taking off — sounds that would further obscure divisions between songs.

Both Knuckles and Levan would watch Siano in awe. His way of mixing records could keep people dancing in a Quaalude-and-fruit-fed frenzy all night long. Siano was brilliant at hit making, and, partly due to him, New York's top dance sounds changed from 1960s soul and Motown to the faster, lusher "Philly soul" sound generated by groups like the Three Degrees and the O'Jays, and by thickly orchestrated instrumental bands like the MFSB Orchestra.

In 1972, Frankie Knuckles and Larry Levan were cutting their teeth playing Philly soul as DJs at a fabulous gay bathhouse named the Continental Baths, which was billed as a "total concept for the sophisticated New York male." It was a dreamy disco lifestyle world housing baths and saunas, a club, bars, a beauty salon, apartment towers, a gym, suntanning terraces, boutiques, a movie theater, and a cabaret stage. Knuckles was impressed by the *gayness* of the place: "It was a fantasy. Everything was up for grabs at the Baths. *Everyone* was up for grabs." Knuckles says that while he was DJing at the Baths, disco music was becoming increasingly thrilling to him. "Around the mid-seventies," he says, "all that new Salsoul music was just so energizing."

The Salsoul label's uptempo dance style — Latin percussion-plus-funk-plus-strings — turned the Philly soul sound into disco. The Salsoul style was as revolutionary as the medium this record label began producing: the twelve-inch single. With this new twelve-inch, maxi-single format, the maxi disco track was born — songs extended by the remix, which allowed DJs like Siano, Knuckles, and Levan much more freedom to mix creatively. When, in 1975, the computer entered the disco picture via electronic-based disco tracks like Giorgio Moroder's Donna Summer productions (notably, the twelve-minute digi-orgasm "I Feel Love"), disco's potential seemed positively endless.

In 1977, *Newsweek* ran a cover story called "Disco Mania." The movie *Saturday Night Fever* was poised to sweep the nation. Everyone, from Rod Stewart to *Star Trek* actor William Shatner, was recording disco records. In Straightsville, disco was mainstreaming fast and would soon experience a great backlash. In the gay enclave, where disco was understood more as a socializing force than a musical style, the story would be altogether different. In 1977, Larry Levan was invited to Chicago to become the resident DJ at a gay disco called the Warehouse, the club that would eventually give house music its name. Levan declined. He was already signed to play at a new New York disco called the Paradise Garage. He suggested to the Warehouse people that they ask Frankie Knuckles instead. With Frankie Knuckles at Chicago's Warehouse and Larry Levan at Manhattan's Paradise Garage, the two heaviest pillars in the construction of house music were in place.

1977–1987: The Paradise Garage, New York City

The Paradise Garage, housed in a converted parking garage in SoHo, was where Larry Levan rose to terrific fame, and it remains the most mythologized of all the New York gay discos. Its memory is still made love to by former patrons, many of whom preserve any remaining scraps of the place — a letter sent out to members, a membership card, coat-check tickets, even straws from the bar — pressing them into pristine albums. Maybe the "Garage Syndrome" is all rose-tinted back-in-the-dayism — some of it surely is — but the strange thing about the Garage is that people had the cajones for the place just as bad when the club was *open.* "The perfect nightclub," wrote journalist Steven Harvey in a 1983 issue of *Collusion* magazine; "the main dance room feel[s] like a rocket at the point of lift-off."

The club officially opened in January of 1977, and it closed in 1987. It benefited from being a latecomer disco: DJs like Nicky Siano had already pioneered the mixing techniques that turned the DJ from entertainer into artist. Larry Levan could take a step forward and turn the DJ — new twelve-inch singles and remixes in hand — into auteur. Garage owner Michael Brody was an old hand at disco and knew exactly what he wanted his club to be: a home. A home mainly for Black and Latino men and their friends, a two-thousand capacity haven from prejudice, a decompression zone, not a place to pose or to have sex in backrooms, but a place to *dance.*

The Garage found its main inspiration in DJ David Mancuso's Loft club, which had been running since 1970 with a similarly homey vibe. The Loft *was* actually Mancuso's home — his large loft apartment, which he opened up for seventy-two hours straight every weekend. The place was filled with balloons, and on offer were spiked punch, free food, masterfully mixed disco-soul, an invitation-only membership ("Loft Babies"), and a lovingly perfected sound system.

The Garage took the Loft idea and made it bigger and better. Noted soundman Richard Long was brought in to codesign the club's speaker system with Levan. Together, they introduced such nightclub innovations as "tweeter arrays," which isolated and enhanced the highs, and special low-end subwoofers, which were so original to the Garage they were dubbed "Larry's Horn." The Loft's invitation-only policy turned into the Garage's members-only policy. People were interviewed; if they passed, they got a membership photo card, which was essential for entry into the club. The Garage opened on Friday and Saturday nights; it closed whenever people left the next morning or afternoon. The policy was never kick the people out. There was free food, lockers for storing changes of clothing, napping areas, and a rooftop terrace to help get members through the six-, eight-, ten-, twelve-hour dance stretch comfortably.

But the main attraction was Levan. Revered like no other DJ before him, he was one of the first "superstar DJs." He was keenly aware of the power a DJ could hold and was infatuated with sound engineering: he always came prepared with three different kinds of needle cartridges for his turntables. Levan would up the quality of the needle (and thus the quality of sound) throughout the night in correspondence with the crowd's frenzy level. When the crowd was close to peaking, at about 5 A.M., Levan would install his best needles, $150 Grace cartridges, saving the greatest boom of sound for when his dancers needed it most.

Levan's DJing style was so intricate that some journalists of the time called it "live remixing." He would layer a cappella vocals over dub bass lines and tease his audience by weaving one record in and out of another track, tweaking the EQ knobs to highlight bits as he went. For him, sound was like plasticine — it could be molded into whatever shape would suit his dancers at a given moment.

The way Levan DJed would become one of the building blocks in the development of house music. The hodgepodge of music that he played at the Garage wasn't classic disco at all. It was something entirely new. Levan seamlessly blended Philly and Salsoul classics with dubbed-out tracks like Dinosaur L's "Go Bang," electrofunk, sound effects, chartpop, reggae, avant-garde computer music like that of German group Kraftwerk, and special edits off reel-to-reel tape, which Levan would create at home especially for the club. By about 1985, Levan was also playing some strange new tracks that were coming out of Chicago — sparse, bass-heavy, stripped-down, electronic disco records. Urban legend has it that upon hearing the first of these records, Levan (who died in 1992 of an AIDS-related illness) called up his old friend Frankie Knuckles in Chicago to ask him where all this crazy stuff was coming from.

1977–1983: Chicago, the Warehouse, and the Dawn of House Music

When Frankie Knuckles first arrived in Chicago in 1977 to take the gig at the gay Black club called the Warehouse, there were only two other clubs in Chicago that actually used DJs instead of jukeboxes. There were no other nightclubs that stayed open after drinking hours. Chicago is a macho city, a bar city, a sports-bar city even. Disco, plus the gay emancipation that came packed within it, took a bit longer to get there. Once there, it stuck — a well-needed pressure valve, especially for Black homosexuals, who had to endure the intense segregation of the American Midwest in addition to the homophobia bred both outside and inside the Black community.

The force of disco became so noticeable in Chicago that in 1979 local rock-radio DJ Steve Dahl organized the now-infamous Disco Demolition Derby at Comiskey Park. It was an extravaganza during which one hundred thousand disco records were dynamited as a halftime show for a heavy Midwester game between the Chicago White Sox and the Detroit Tigers. The explosion ignited a riot among the baseball fans, who came streaming onto the field to celebrate their disco hatred and, indirectly, or maybe very directly, their homophobia. But, notwithstanding this event, Chicago DJs of the Black underground will tell you that theirs is a city in which disco has refused to die.

Knuckles's choice of music in his first few years at the Warehouse was not completely different from Levan's at the Garage — the meat of the night was composed of Philly and Salsoul sounds spliced with a grab bag of other genres. But Knuckles's playlist was a bit more disco-classicist than Levan's. Knuckles would never mix in Van Halen records or obscurist-weirdo Euro avant-garde fare the way Levan did. Knuckles was very fond of the vocals that could be found in 1977–78 disco: the inspirational or devotional messages of records like D-Train's "Keep On."

But as the eighties neared, few people were recording songs like these any more. The record industry had pronounced disco "dead," and major labels were losing their dance departments. Much of America's urban Black underground was turning on to the burgeoning street sounds of rap and electro. At risk of becoming a retro DJ, Knuckles had to get creative with his favorite records.

He began to do dramatic live alterations of disco songs. Like Levan, he would slice, dice, and make the most of homemade reel-to-reel edits — stretching out drum breaks or extracting a cappella vocals. Soon Knuckles was also messing about with the newly affordable Japanese drum machines, setting down rhythm tracks to beef up his existing records, running kick drums or bolstered bass underneath key songs. This fattening-up technique drove the crowds wild, especially when Knuckles would let the record drop out altogether, leaving only the drum-machine sequence playing on its own. The punters at the Warehouse called Knuckles's style "Warehouse music." Sometimes they shortened this to "house music."

By 1983, other gay, Black after-hours discos like the Warehouse were cropping up in Chicago, and Knuckles's "house" DJing style was catching on. R&B station WBMX began featuring DJ-mix shows by the Hot Mix 5, five Warehouse-inspired DJs including one named Farley "Jackmaster" Funk and another called Steve "Silk" Hurley. The Hot Mix 5 shows were said to have lured close to one million people around this time — one fifth of Chicago's population. With Chicago's musicscape opening up to DJs, Knuckles moved on to a newer club, the Powerplant. Nearby, Knuckles's nemesis, a new-kid-in-town DJ named Ron Hardy, was playing at a club called the Music Box. "Knuckles was a smooth DJ; Hardy was raw as fuck," says Chicago house-producer Cajmere. "Ron Hardy gave this music its insanity, its all-night freak-out aspect, and Knuckles was the more *linear* side of things. The Powerplant was cool. But Ron Hardy and the Music Box? It was ghetto, man! The next level!"

At Knuckles's Powerplant, a suave house dress code was emerging: Afros snipped into boxy "fade" and flat-top haircuts crowning an urbanized English-riding sartorial style complete with jodhpurs, tweeds, broaches, and sometimes even a riding crop. At the Music Box, where drug use was rampant and sex was in the air, the fashion was raunchy-punky dress-to-sweat: Harem pants, loose clothing, leather, double wraparound stud belts, and hair dyed bright colors. Both clubs were becoming increasingly mixed but with an undilutable gay core. If you were gay, you were called a "child." If you were straight, a "stepchild." Frankie Knuckles says that in these clubs it actually became fashionable to be gay. "Well, I think some people were experimenting with their sexuality a lot back then," he remarks. "It was a way to be in with the 'in crowd' and closer to the music, I suppose."

No longer the only spinner in town, Knuckles had become involved in a game of one-upmanship with Hardy and several other Chicago jocks: who could do weirder, crazier things to records; who could mix, phase, cut, strip, and edit records up into such a storm that the original song became secondary to what you did to it.

Chicago DJs were soon going into the studio to make their own DJ-aid recordings, using the facilities to bolster their mixes and their originality. Shortly thereafter, clubbers started getting into it too. "Everybody saw how easy it was to make one of these tracks using drum machines and samplers and stuff," says Knuckles. These tracks, usually recorded onto tape, often consisted of nothing more than a bass line and some drum patterns. In a matter of months, the producers of these tapes began adding samples, effects, and more melody. When, in 1983, Jesse Saunders and Vince Lawrence's tape "On & On" (a stripped-down interpretation of the Salsoul classic by First Choice) was committed to vinyl, the first house record was officially pressed.

1983–1987: Chicago House and Detroit Techno

The success of "On & On," which sold thousands in Chicago, catalyzed producers and entrepreneurs alike. Soon Chicago had two house labels, DJ International and Trax. By 1986, generally thought of as "the year house broke," these labels had brought several house hits to the American underground club scene. One of the first was Farley "Jackmaster" Funk's "Jack Your Body," which featured a strange, irregular kick drum, romper pianos, and an eerie, staccato sample that urged dancers to "j-j-j-jack your body." Another biggie was "Love Can't Turn Around," by Marshall Jefferson and Jesse Saunders, featuring singer Darryl Pandy, which paired the computerized percussion of the young house sound with gospelly vocals.

By 1987, house movers in Chicago no longer viewed their art as merely the reformatting of disco. Interest was beginning to shift away from the seminal art of my-mix-is-crazier-than-yours DJing and towards producing. With house solidly understood in Chicago as its own genre, a *new* kind of music, studio experimentation increased tremendously. Producer Larry Heard created a more moody and "deep" style of house music through tracks like "Washing Machine." Singer Jamie Principle recorded "Baby Wants to Ride," a spooky-bloopy house track featuring Principle whispering little erotic nothings ("I want to fuck you! Whoo! All night long"), which would lead to a durable minigenre of Moroder-informed orgasmo-house.

Most influential on a global scale, however, was a record by a group of producers who called themselves Phuture, led by a Chicago kid named DJ Pierre. One night, Pierre came across a "crazy frequency sound" while playing around with a Roland TB

303 Bass Line machine in his home studio. Tweaking and turning knobs while this frequency was running on the 303, Pierre created a freakazoided, undulating, gurgling, psychedelic, wah-wah effect. The final result of his discovery was Phuture's record "Acid Tracks." It was the first of numerous acid house records that would use the Roland TB 303 (a machine originally intended to provide bass lines for practicing guitarists) in this unconventional way.

The fresh DIY-ism of Chicago's musical production was catching on. By the mid-eighties, home-studio house music from New York, New Jersey, and Washington was also being made and independently pressed. In 1986, British A&R men who had traveled to Chicago to sign up house producers had also discovered another locus of activity quite close by. Some Chicago DJs had told them that a few of the key house-club records were actually the products of another Midwestern city — Detroit.

Since the sixties, Detroit has remained one of the more depressed cities in America. Detroit's club scene was virtually nonexistent next to Chicago's, and so Detroit-area dance music tended to sound much less sweaty-physical. The main authors of the pristine Detroit sound were friends Juan Atkins, Derrick May, and Kevin Saunderson, three straight, Black, middle-class teens hailing not from the inner city but from an affluent suburb called Belleville.

This trio was involved in a little DJing company called Deep Space. As there were no clubs in the region, the Deep Space DJs had their work cut out for them. They threw parties for their peers (members of a Black, fashion-conscious, high-school circle they called the "GQ set") in empty spaces, restaurants, and school gymnasiums. Deep Space played mainly European synthesizer pop, from Depeche Mode and Gary Numan to avant-garde fare like Kraftwerk. "All that European synth music, man, that was our thing," says Derrick May. "It was just classy and clean, and to us it was beautiful, like outer space. Living around

Detroit, there was so little beauty . . . everything is an ugly mess in Detroit, and so we were attracted to this music. It, like, ignited our imagination!"

Juan Atkins, the oldest of the Belleville trio, was obsessed with the future and with outer space, introducing May and Saunderson to books like Alvin Toffler's *Third Wave* and movies like *Blade Runner*. Prior to doing the Deep Space parties, Atkins, in 1981, began recording electro music as part of the duo Cybotron. "I wanted to make music that sounded like it was made by computers and machines," he says — "like advanced future music." By the mid-eighties, Atkins had set up a record label called Metroplex and had invited his friends to record music, too. Influenced by trips they had taken to Chicago, Atkins, May, and Saunderson combined a clubby sway with *Blade Runner*-ish ideas about what the next millenium might sound like and their love of frigid European synth music. Their final product sounded very much like what you'd imagine house music would sound like if it had been made by Germans in the mid-eighties: sharp and industrial. "God, we lived right next to an industrial cesspool," says May. "Of course our music sounded harder and mechanical . . . like machine soul music."

Those visiting British A&R men realized that it would be hard to package the Detroit music they were hearing as house: it was colder and more electronicky, its lineage was not disco, and it was more obviously conceptualized; also, in 1986, the word *house* was inextricably linked to the word *Chicago*. Instead, everyone agreed it would be better to go along with the name the Belleville trio had already given their own sound. "We were calling it techno," says May. "Nobody gave us that name. I think it was just the obvious title for the kind of music we made."

1987–1990: Ecstasy and the London Acid-House Scene

In 1987, the word in Chicago and in the underground house clubs that were spreading into major North American cities was that in England house was *really* successful, not just an underground thing. In January of 1987, Farley's "Jack Your Body" had reached number one, and other Chicago house records were reaching the top twenty, too. Yet the American rumor was an overstatement: house may have been charting in England, but only as a faddish thing, a novelty music, almost. It was being played in a few clubs and at certain illegal warehouse parties, but the sound was proving difficult to introduce — by no means was it "taking over." A particularly telling slice is a list of the top one hundred trends of 1987 compiled by British style-bible magazine *i-D* and published in the January 1988 issue: Minneapolis funker Prince is number one; rare groove is number ten; house music is number forty-eight.

Rare groove is the name of the club sound and scene that house eventually superseded in London. "Rare groove was the snobbiest thing ever," says Push, founder and former editor of the British dance-music monthly *Muzik*, who, in the late eighties, was covering the club scene for music weeklies *Sounds* and *Melody Maker*. "It was all DJs playing the most obscure American soul and funk they could find, hiding their record labels so that other DJs couldn't see them, a total elitist SoHo scene, with dress codes and special dances and exclusivity written all over it. In a way, it was the British class system ingested and spit out again . . . England's worst exclusionary side made into a club scene. When the acid-house [scene] came up, it was the end of all that."

The acid-house scene was the first fully glued British culture in which house music was a major player. The term "acid house" used as a description for the early British house scene is something that has often been misunderstood in North America, both then and now. In America, "acid house" refers to the specific sound of house music that incorporates the TB 303 gurgle noise, and "house" is the term for the dance culture from which these sounds emanate. In England, while "acid house" refers to the TB 303 sound, too (Phuture's "Acid Trax" proved inordinately influential in the UK, spawning many British copycat tracks), the term is also widely used to describe the country's entire house culture of the years 1988 and 1989. To make a long story short, in the British acid-house scene, all sorts of housey styles were played — from Chicago records to British DJ records like M/A/R/R/S's "Pump up the Volume." "I think the naming of the movement was just off the cuff, really," says Push. "In 1988, people started calling anything that sounded 'crazy' acid house. The drug reference in the term was cool, too."

The drug of the acid house movement in Britain was not, of course, LSD. It was another illegal substance called MDMA — Ecstasy — which was to become known in the UK as "E." The drug MDMA (3, 4–methylenedioxymethylamphetamine), illegal in the UK since 1970, was patented by the German pharmaceutical firm Merck in 1914. Merck is now believed to have experimented with the drug until the early 1920s, trying to find different uses for it. But the company never actually marketed MDMA, and the drug was quite forgotten until the 1970s, when a group of New Agey American psychotherapists began experimenting with it. They had tapped in to MDMA's great inhibition-releasing powers and were using the drugs to treat those in marriage counseling and people suffering from anxiety or depression.

The substance soon found its way into New York gay clubs like the Saint and the Paradise Garage under the street name Ecstasy. Clubbers often shortened this to "X" or "XTC" or "E." It was also available during the early eighties in certain circles in London's West End — yuppies and the patrons of a couple of fashion-scene clubs used it. These early recreational users considered Ecstasy to be more of a mellow, "bonding drug" than a dance drug.

The first place Ecstasy was used as a mass dance drug was Texas. There, it surfaced at glamorous nighteries like Dallas's Starck Club. At the Starck, Ecstasy was legally sold over the counter (you could charge it on a credit card if you liked) from about 1982 until 1985, when MDMA was designated a Schedule 1 drug by the US government — as illegal as heroin or cocaine. "Ecstasy took our inhibitions down," says Wade Hampton, a regular at Dallas Ecstasy clubs. "We knew Ecstasy had been around with yuppies and stuff, but we couldn't believe nobody had thought of dancing on this drug before. It made music sound so good, it made dancing in a club feel like a great uniting, important action."

The drug MDMA acts on a brain chemical called serotonin, which is said to play an important part in shaping mood, thought processes, sleeping patterns, eating patterns, reaction to external stimuli, and control of motor activity. Still very little is known about serotonin, but low levels of that brain chemical are generally believed to be associated with depression. Serotonin is a neurotransmitter, transferring messages across the synapses (or gaps) between adjacent neurons (nerve cells). Ingesting MDMA causes an increase in levels of serotonin, which then floods into the synapses. The drug also affects the reabsorption of serotonin into neurons, creating something of a wild serotonin party in the brain.

The effects of a pure MDMA pill can last several hours, usually from four to six. The drug will take hold after thirty to forty-five minutes, introducing itself with little waves of excitement, which are often accompanied by an uncomfortable feeling in the stomach or a panicky disorientation. These effects are generally quelled soon afterwards by a feeling of intense well-being, both sensual (music sounds better, touching feels nicer, things look clearer, and tastes and smells seem stronger) and emotional (empathy, loosened inhibitions, a sense of bonding with others, and often happiness or even euphoria). In short, Ecstasy makes you feel "loved up."

The brainwave of Ecstasy-as-dance-drug did not reach London via Texans on vacation. It came through a bunch of scraping-by London DJs who were spending their summers on Ibiza, one of

Spain's Balearic Islands. Since the sixties, Ibiza had been a heavenly, unspoiled resort divided into two territories. On one side, hippies, travelers, and artists congregated. On the other, the New Agey rich and famous (Grace Jones, members of Pink Floyd) tended to gather. It was on the latter side that the London DJs found a lush, open-air disco called Amnesia, where house was mixed with indie rock, flamenco, and what-you-like. They also found a drug called Ecstasy, which had come to Ibiza with the regular influx of New Age yuppies.

"The [DJs] came back in the fall of 1987. They had all taken their first Ecstasy trips in this hippie-ish, under-the-stars, beautiful, open vibe, and wanted to re-create it," says Push. "They weren't trendy DJs at the time. They didn't have major clout or anything. But they got back to London, it was probably raining, and they wanted their summer magic back, so they started doing these Ibiza revival nights, playing this Balearic mix, and finding Ecstasy from the few dealers in London or connections back [in Ibiza] to go along with it."

The three most Ibiza-mad of this DJing lot were Danny Rampling, Paul Oakenfold, and Nicky Holloway. Each of them created club nights in London. Rampling set up one called Shoom (in December 1987), Oakenfold started one called Spectrum (in April 1988), and Holloway created one called the Trip (in June 1988). In London, it was through these three club nights, along with the important adjuncts of rawer warehouse parties, that the ideas of house music, Balearic New Age hippieness, and the drug Ecstasy smashed into each other, creating the acid-house explosion of the summer of 1988 — what some in England still refer to as the "Summer of Love."

Shoom originally took place in a gym called the Fitness Center, located just south of the Thames. Of the three newfangled club nights, Shoom was the one most rife with the Technicolor back-to-the-sixties, back-to-the-garden, back-to-the-age-of-love idealism that characterized acid house's first summer. "People were so overwhelmed by this new, open, druggy, psychedelic atmosphere," says Push. "I think the closest thing they could compare it to was what they may have thought the sixties were like. Places like Shoom were packed with a kind of cartoon hippie thing."

The have-a-nice-day yellow smiley face was appropriated as the Shoom symbol. People wore loose, summery Ibiza-style clothes to Shoom: Converse All Star sneakers, John Lennon glasses, bandannas, hand-painted (often smiley-emblazoned) T-shirts, fabrics with printed patterns, ponchos, shorts, all crowned with a unisex ponytail. They spoke of peace and love, of changing the world. Danny Rampling, who ran Shoom with his wife, Jenni, would buy ice lollies and other treats for their patrons. Sometimes the Ramplings filled the Shoom space with strawberry-flavored smoke.

"That smoke! You couldn't even see an inch in front of you at Shoom!" says Mark Moore, one of the first DJs to try introducing house to London. In 1988, Moore also hit number one in the UK as part of housey duo S'Express. "When dancing at Shoom, all you could do was fall into your own trance. It was so different from what was going on in London before. The eighties were considered the 'style decade' in this city. It was all see and be seen. At Shoom, it was almost as if overnight everything changed. All of a sudden, the people who were the coolest a month before seemed *sooo* unbelievably *out*."

The use of Ecstasy — which was still quite hard to come by at this point — was creating some new and curious customs. "People would just come up to you and hug you, smiling like mad, asking if you were enjoying your night," says Nick Spiers, a regular Shoom-goer. "Shoomers brought toys and silly things like whistles into the club — it seems stupid now, but then it was all about this huggyness, this childlike aspect of taking E for the first time and being reborn. It was amazing. In England, people did not usually hug strangers and things like that."

Yet, for all its claims of happy-happy openness, Shoom was notoriously hard to get into. It occupied a small physical space, and only an elite of Ibiza graduates, friends, and friends of friends were admitted. While Shoom was included week after week in listings magazines like *Time Out*, no address was given and the blurbs were rife with insiderspeak and allusion to the fact that only "those in the know" could pass through the Shoom gates. "There was a feeling among the people at Shoom," says Nick Spiers, "that if too many found out about it, it would ruin things. Shoom was so special and optimistic, we really felt like we had discovered the secret of the ages."

"But the thing is, this *thing* touched a nerve in London," says Push. "We were going on ten years of Thatcherism and a government who didn't give a shit about this country's youth. Everybody I knew grew up with this total hatred of Thatcherism but at the same time felt completely unable to do anything about it — there was just this feeling of no hope. England's youth needed release and escape. This new club thing could not stay a secret."

When Paul Oakenfold launched Spectrum in the gigantic Heaven club at Charing Cross on a Monday night, his friends thought he was half mad. Monday is the deadest night of the clubbing week. Nothing works on a Monday. "Within three weeks, there were two thousand people in the club, and more waiting outside every Monday," says Push. Spectrum was less hand-painted Ibiza and more psychedelic — to the point of being maniacal: it was filled with lasers and strobe lights and explosions of confetti. The subtitle of the Spectrum flyer was "Theater of Madness." In correspondence, the British taste in house seemed to be getting madder and more theatrical. Connections to house's disco roots and even connections to sun-kissed Ibiza, were weakening under the throbbing, freaky beats of new acidic anthems: from British productions like S'Express's "Theme from S'Express," to warbling Chicago productions like Fast Eddie's "Acid Thunder," to the Jungle Brothers' manic rap-house corker

"I'll House You." Punters at Spectrum would dance with arms like airplane propellers gone bonkers, hands in the air, chanting what was to become the dance-floor rallying cry of summer 1988: "aciiied!"

The success of Spectrum rubbed some of the Shoomers and original Balearic crew the wrong way. The bonhomie and "family vibe" of the Ramplings' acid ideal was being lost within Spectrum's "theater of madness." The secret of Ecstasy was out. Soon, smiley T-shirts and rings and shoelaces and whistles became available in cheapo-reapo teenybopper chain stores like Top Shop. Newspapers were catching onto the new culture, still oblivious to the drug angle of the story. Major-label compilations promoted the flashy woopi-woopi sirens of British acid tracks like D-Mob's "We Call It Aciied" over anything authentically Balearic. But, worst of all, *suburbanites* were moving in. The folk devil of the "acid ted" was soon created by the old school, an acid ted being a working-class yobo or a clueless middle-classer who necks Es and dances to acid wearing too many smiley accessories with no idea *why*.

Nicky Holloway's the Trip has been the least-mythologized and most-derided of the three famous 1988 acid clubs. A Saturday club night in the hulking Astoria venue off Tottenham Court Road, the Trip was the first acid-ted club, the one that accommodated rival football hooligans hugging on Ecstasy ("Love Thugs"), uncool "sheep" drenched in smileys, and suburban Sharons 'n' Traceys who'd swapped their white pumps for fluorescent sneakers. The Trip was the largest, most obvious, and ultimately the most crazed of the 1988 club triumvirate. Banners were hung along the Astoria's walls bearing words like *drugs* and *acid*. Ecstasy was readily available at the Trip, and patrons would still be on a full-blown high when closing time arrived. They'd stream out onto Tottenham Court Road and party to the sound of car stereos. When the police came — and they always did — the Trippers would start dancing to the sound of the police sirens, chanting "Aciied!!" and "Can you feel iiiiiiit?!" after Todd Terry's siren-filled house anthem "Can You Party."

1989–1992: The British Rave Boom

It was the acid teds who ultimately, in 1989, took acid house to the next level. These johnny-come-latelies, these "sheep," carried acid house outside the clubs, bringing it with them to parties of tens of thousands held in airplane hangars, warehouses, and, most remarkably, the fields surrounding the ring-around-London M25 orbital highway.

Throughout 1988, acid housers sometimes described what they were doing in clubs as "raving." In 1989, this sometimes-used term became fully loaded: raving became something done by ravers at these new, illegal parties — raves. "By the end of 1988, every fucking club in the city was doing acid-house night, the word *acid* had become really dirty, yet people still wanted more," says Push. "You didn't need to be the keenest of entrepreneurs to see that what was happening in London could have been happening on a much larger scale.

Tony Colston-Hayter, the most famous orbital-rave promoter ever, was, in fact, a keen entrepreneur. While still in high school, he set up a million-dollar computer-game hire service. Once out of school, he became a professional blackjack player of some note. He and his soon-to-be partner in promotions, Dave Roberts, frequented the Trip in 1988. Inspired, they began throwing acid warehouse parties at Wembley Studios under the name Apocalypse Now. These parties were a smash, and when ITV's *News at Ten* contacted Colston-Hayter about doing a piece on his good fortune he accepted. The *News at Ten* piece did not actually end up focusing on Colston-Hayter's capitalist flair; instead, it featured drug dealers, ravers screaming into cameras, and Do-you-know-where-your-children-are? scare tactics. The moral panic that had been steadily building in the mainstream media after the honeymoon summer of 1988 was now cranked up high. The London Metropolitan Police were not going to sit idle for much longer while people danced to their sirens. So, if acid house was to continue growing, it needed to get the hell outta town.

Promoter Colston-Hayter, immediately categorized by the Shoomey old school as the ultimate "chancer promoter" (the "in-it-for-the-money" ringmaster of the acid teds), changed his company's name to Sunrise. In the fall of 1988, he rented a fleet of buses for his first country rave, the Sunrise Mystery Trip, which would take his ravers from London to the mossy green landscape of Buckinghamshire. Colston-Hayter's idea was to turn the confined clubland of acid house into a vast til-dawn fantasticland getaway for thousands of adults. At the Mystery Trip site, he furnished such Ecstasy-friendly accoutrements as a bouncy inflatable castle where shoeless ravers could jump around like kiddies on Mum's big bed.

The same week as Sunrise's first party, England's second (but up to that point most publicized) Ecstasy-related death occurred. The media flew into a predictable frenzy, and the police/governmental reaction was extreme; the authorities became determined to shut down the raves at any cost. Yet orbital raves spread through 1989. Sunrise copycat companies like Energy, Biology, and World Dance vied with one another, each trying to manufacture the ultimate one-night playground for E users. "Some of these raves would get twenty thousand people at them. It felt like the whole of England was raving and doing E," says Push. Rave had come to signify not just an acceptance but a celebration of the mass. Excited murmuring about rave being the biggest British youth eruption since the sixties was everywhere. People who would have never set foot in a West End club were out raving in full force. Many of them had first learned about the scene through titillating tabloid scare stories on the dangers of Ecstasy and the "horror" of these parties.

It was as if the very illegality of rave became a unifying force among ravers. A cat-and-mouse routine between rave promoters and the police ensued. As 1989 progressed, parties became increasingly hard to find; schemes involving map points and site changes and info-giving mobile phone numbers were employed by promoters. "You could spend a whole night in your car, driving around in circles, seeing other ravers along the way, and asking *them* if they knew where the rave was," says Push. "Sometimes you would finally find the party site just as it was being shut down by the police. Sometimes groups of people would just give up, park in a rest stop, crank their car stereos and create miniraves along the [highway]. But, for a time, this chase aspect became part of the fun."

When the authorities finally chased the wind out of the orbital-rave scene, the culture began fragmenting. By early 1990, the acid-age old school had deemed rave "dead" and left for good, towing the music press and style press with them. They began setting up a "glam," unravey urban house scene, building "quality" clubs like London's luxurious Ministry of Sound. A second wave of ravers entered the rave arena. The old school, and even those involved in the orbital scene, called these newbies "cheesy quavers" — the acid teds of the nineties, but even later off the mark.

"The new ravers were younger and there were loads more of them. More ravers than ever," says Push. "Rave just became terribly uncool. A suburban teen scene. I think it had more of a low-class aura to it." The rave scene did, indeed, grow to monstrous proportions, due to its new accessible status. In order to survive police actions, one-off raves had to go "corporate" — legal and licensed. Second-wave rave promoters popped up across the UK, companies like Rezerection and Raindance. In addition to this, many massive rave clubs were set up in suburbia. Stripped of all its underground secrecy, the scene attracted a crowd less concerned with tastemaking or ideological brouhaha and more concerned with the practicalities of getting really screwed on drugs and dancing like a loon for ten hours straight. "Drug use upped tremendously," says Push. "People were taking five, six, seven, ten, twenty pills a night. It was almost as if these new [ravers], many of them coming from hard backgrounds, felt like they had nothing to lose."

Like many other street drugs, Ecstasy has a honeymoon period followed by a comedown period. In the honeymoon period, drug purity is high, one pill does what it should, payback is low. In the comedown period, drug purity begins to disintegrate, people begin doing things like stacking pills, and payback can become grisly, sometimes even outweighing pleasure.

Because by 1990 many of rave's original seats of power and controlling infrastructures had evaporated, ample space was left for scamming. A lot of what was being sold as Ecstasy was not, in fact, MDMA. There were aspirin and ephedrine (the stuff found in hay-fever medications like Sudafed). There were cocktails of LSD, ketamine, caffeine, talcum powder, and what-you-like. There were MDEA and MDA, cousins to MDMA with effects different from Ecstasy's. There were rumors of crushed glass and heroine and rat-poison tablets — more fiction than fact. But, most significantly, there was speed: amphetamine.

In one respect, speed's infiltration of the British rave scene is not dissimilar to the drug's penetration of the Haight-Ashbury hippie scene at the tail end of the sixties. In both cases, speed sidled in alongside drugs considered mind-expanding — LSD in the hippie scene, MDMA in rave — when the culture they were associated with began edging away from its roots. In the case of rave, speed, along with the hodgepodge of other chemicals sold as Ecstasy, actually accelerated this alienation process, if only through the acceleration of rave music's beats-per-minute. The average BPM of a classic house song is somewhere around 125. The average BPM of the music favored in the second-wave rave era is an astounding 150–170.

This supersonic, speed-mad music was called "hardcore

techno." By 1990, *techno* had become something of a catch-all term denoting anything less traditionally soulful than house, usually faster, and often European. Hardcore techno was the first fully fledged genre of British rave music. A sound tailor-made for rave. Its sonic roots were manifold, with influences to be found everywhere, from the Belgian rave scene (which had its own, different version of hardcore techno) to the basement studios of future-finding American producers like Joey Beltram.

A London club called Rage was extremely important in the development of this music. At Rage, resident DJ duo Fabio and Grooverider was conducting experiments with the velocity of house music as early as 1989. They had taken to playing certain house records at forty-five RMP instead of thirty-three — specifically, house records that employed breakbeats, the syncopated drum patterns usually associated with funk and hip-hop, the boom-b-BOOM, boom-boom-b-BOOM beat (as opposed to classic house's or disco's straight 4/4 beat — boom-boom-boom). These breakbeat records — like those by East London duo Shut Up and Dance — were often assisted by very low bass lines, the kind you'd expect from dub or reggae sound systems. When this bass-drenched techno-on-45 sound was pressed onto vinyl (vocals sped up to sound like chipmunks, and so on) by labels like Suburban Base, British hardcore techno was officially born.

To many outsiders, the densely populated hardcore rave scene seemed like a degraded, even scary, freakzone of E-crunching prole monsters jogging in place to ridiculous gimmicky music. A place of Ecstasy rituals gone bonkers. Hardcore ravers wore white gloves or fluorescent strips to trip off the lasers. They smeared their torsos with Vick's Vaporub to maximize the tingling of the E buzz. They even slathered Vaporub into surgical masks (sometimes decorated with a hand-painted "E," just in case someone should miss the point) and inhaled the mentholated stuff all night.

The kiddiness of whistles and toys first seen at Shoom spun into a complete aesthetic of juvenilia: hardcore ravers took to biting down on pacifiers instead of chewing gum to control the "gurning" — the quivering jaw their speedy Es brought on. Kiddie party accessories like glo-sticks and noisemakers like tambourines were suddenly all the rage; skinny hardcore ravers, emaciated from weekend after weekend of nutter dancing and drugs, took to sporting xxx-large T-shirts and woolly hats emblazoned with back-to-kindergarten images like Dennis the Menace, Cookie Monster, and cereal boxes.

Yet, despite its reputation of being a messy kiddie mess, hardcore rave was actually the most complete, homegrown, and well-oiled rave culture England ever made. Hardcore was self-sufficient. It made its own music (music that didn't fly in from America on an airplane). Its fashions and rituals were completely internally derived. And, in a youth-media blackout zone, hardcore even had its own intricate modes of communication: flyers became more extravagant, featuring long lists of DJs, shout outs, infolines, plus anything else that could be crammed onto one multicolored paper square of party advertising. Hardcore even had its own micropress in zines like *Ravescene Magazeen*.

By 1992, hardcore rave also had its own musical overground and underground. On the commercial end, a teenybopper-amusement-parkish hardcore kept slamming onto the pop charts, even with next to no help from commercial radio: the Prodigy's 1991 anthem "Charly," or Smart E's *Sesame Street* rip-off "Sesame's Treet," or Acen's 1992 kids-in-space squeal-a-thon "Trip to the Moon," best remembered for its helium-fed refrain, "Take me higher." On the underground end, pirate radio came back to life in the hardcore era, with illegal London stations like Centre Force playing darker, more bass-heavy strains of the music, a sound that would eventually lead to the music called "jungle."

1990–1993: Storm Raves and the Development of an American Rave Scene

In a way, hardcore seems like it would have been the most tricky style of British house culture to export, simply because it was *sooo* innately British — created through a particularly British experience, soundtracked by mainly British music, and influenced by dodgy British drugs. It was geared to what they were going through "over there." "Import hardcore to America?" asks the Prodigy's Liam Howlett when speaking of his attitude in the early nineties. "I guess we just figured there was no way Americans could understand it. It was too far gone."

Yet somehow it was bits of the hardcore rave aesthetic that caught North America's fancy earliest (except in a few notable locations like San Francisco). Because it was *big*. Because it was flamboyant. And because it had many fun and immediately identifiable symbols: humongous parties, pacifiers, Vaporub, kiddie graphics, xxx-large clothes, and the letter "E" painted, bolded, and highlighted wherever possible. Maybe some early rave makers in America (barring the many who were expat Britons) couldn't understand where these symbols came from or why. But they could rent warehouses and put bouncy castles in them. And kids could wear *Sesame Street* T-shirts, suck on pacifiers, and dance with glo-sticks. Then they could try Ecstasy and begin figuring out these rituals for themselves. Which they did, fairly swiftly.

Boingy-boingy-boingy British hardcore techno — along with a sprinkling of more severe Belgian-style techno — served as the introductory rave sound in lots of North American cities. Hardcore quickly evaporated in most of these places, to be replaced by music more in tune with whatever the local vibe was. But the outrageous records of hardcore outfits like the Prodigy and sl2 or Belgium's Human Resource served an initial purpose other than simply providing something to dance to for Ameri-rave scenes. Because this music was so far removed from the original gay-Black house model, to many Americans it did not sound even remotely related to house at all — which, for some new rave-scene makers, was just the point.

A big point. In cities like New York, where house clubs were already entrenched, still mostly conforming to the original gay-Black model, the usually White, mainly straight, ravers wanted to differentiate themselves. The "Disco Sucks" tradition had never died in North America, and, in a funny way, parts of early American rave culture can be seen as falling into this antidisco thing. I remember that in my hometown of Montreal, Canada, the first DJs to uphold rave and European techno music printed up T-shirts proclaiming "House Is Dead. Techno Lives" on the front, and "Hardcore You Know the Score," a popular British battle cry of 1991–92, on the back.

It should be noted here that house never really broke out of the undergrounds of cosmopolitan American cities during the eighties the way it did in England. In the early nineties, the North American music industry and the media looked to grunge music as the next big thing, and American house music was pretty much ignored. Chicago's scene had withered by then, but (New York City was reinstated as the US dance capital) and the American house scene swiftly came to terms with its situation. Housers ended up wearing their obscurity as a badge of pride: house wasn't a sellout, it wasn't commercial — it was deep, it was underground. So underground, it didn't reach many of the less-sophisticated centers like Orlando, Florida, or Milwaukee, Wisconsin. In some of these places, British-style raving was the first taste the locals would have of any sort of house-derived culture. Basically, rendered straight 'n White, this thing could go places Black 'n gay could not.

Rave would become something of a hick-town's revenge in America by the mid-nineties, but the first-ever North American rave scene was actually set up in New York. Not within the elder house scene — more like beside it. The importer was an outspoken Italian-American, a maverick Brooklyn DJ and producer named Frankie Bones. Bones began producing dance music in 1987. Some of his records, notably the *Bonesbreak* series of breakbeat house tracks, had won him a bit of status overseas. In 1989, during the heyday of Britain's orbital-rave scene, he had been asked to England to DJ at an Energy rave. Thrilled in the first place to get a free trip to England, Bones got an even bigger thrill when he headed into the Energy DJ booth — with his tough-guy leather jacket and his mulleted hair — and discovered he couldn't see the end of the human sea: before him were twenty-five thousand people in fluo, stripey ravey gear. Bones took his first E on this trip to England. Arriving home — totally gobsmacked by what he'd seen and experienced — he was set on importing this double-wow crazy-rave idea to Brooklyn.

Bones's first gatherings were just little hardcore-soundtracked parties involving a tight nucleus of bridge-and-tunnel kids. The group of friends helping Bones run the show grew into a thick posse: DJs Adam X (Bones's brother), Lenny Dee, Jimmy Crash, promoter Dennis the Menace, and Heather Heart, publisher of America's first rave zine, *Under One Sky*. Sometimes they'd set up a strobe and a sound system in a Brooklyn or Queens warehouse or at some outdoor locale; sometimes they'd even play videos of British raves so that everyone could see exactly how this raving thing was done. Everyone tried Ecstasy for the first time, and the results were predictably lovey. In this era, Bones himself often seemed as if he was on a softy-soft E cloud. In 1991, he began writing a column for the Canadian dance magazine *Streetsound*, in which he spoke of people "coming together," of the power of music, of the true, spiritual meaning of rave.

This Brooklyn period of British mimesis and billowing one-love did not last long. If the history of rave proves anything, it's that the rave format is wide open to interpretation and sculpted by set and setting. By 1992, Bones's hardcore parties were luring thousands of kids and taking on distinctly Brooklynese shapes.

England could have its Raindances; these parties were called Storm Raves. And they were tough. They took place on construction sites, in brickyards, in derelict stables. Kids didn't boogie — they pogod and thrashed. A "wall of sound" tradition was implemented: the more speakers, the louder, the better. The music was moving towards stomping brutal German and Lowlands techno and away from the happy-slappy Brit stuff.

The police got onto things fast, and so Storm Raves — which were happening monthly by 1992 — would either take place in a zone accessible only via a series of map points, or Bones would have some harebrained tale ready for the police when they showed. Sometimes he'd brandish paperwork and tell them that they were in the process of filming something — a live thing, like, um, a concert scene. That explained all the people and noise. Bones's outlook on raves and techno music was becoming increasingly fierce and original; his attitude was part Vinnie Barbarino and part Mafia don. "I refuse to go to jail for having fun. I will always stand for the true meaning of the rave scene," he wrote in the November 1993 *Streetsound*. "My middle name isn't peace. . . . My advice to anyone is stick to your guns . . . and . . . please use real bullets."

A certain gangland element and harder drugs, like PCP and crack cocaine, began filtering into the Storm scenario in 1993. At this point, rave was also firmly entrenched in New York City proper. There, dark-horse rave-baron Lord Michael had brought rave into nightworld-magnate Peter Gatien's clubs the Limelight and the Palladium. "The competition was fierce for awhile — Brooklyn versus NYC, and then New York won out," says "Joey," a Brooklyn native who frequented the Storm raves from 1992 to 1993. "Promoters from Limelight would come to Storm Rave with a really good batch of E and sell it to everyone, get everybody super, super into this amazing stuff, and then give out flyers for Limelight, telling us there's plenty more of this good stuff at Limelight. Then you'd go to Limelight and the E would be shit.

[Limelight-affiliated people] also started calling the police on Storm Raves. That was how the whole empire of New York City rave was started. Dirty cash, dirty intentions."

It was in the NYC rave clubs — like Lord Michael's ventures or NASA, which was run by promoters Scotto and DB — that the neatly designed Ameri-raver stereotype emerged. Ameri-ravers gobbled too many Es. They said "dude" a lot and spoke of "PLUR" (peace, love, unity, respect). They pierced the dickens out of their bodies. They got tattoos. Based on British hardcore style, skateboarder fashion, old-school hip-hop, and preschool favorites, their dress code consisted of pixie skirts, fuzzy-animal rucksacks, pigtails, and baby-Ts for girls; for guys, there were woolly hats and long wallet chains dangling off the side of fatter-than-fat phat pants. And pacifiers for everyone. A distinctive rave-kid dance was developing, too. Not the Brooklyn pogo, or the British-style jog-punch combo, but a kind of sub-break-dancing robot-making-boxes wind-'n-skip.

On the nutter scale, the stylistics of the NYC rave punter were almost outweighed by those of the new, cartoon-worthy techno-rave DJS. There was "America's first techno star," Moby, a vegan-Christian DJ. Or DJ Repete, who published his own comic strip about his crazy rave adventures. Or DJ Keoki, a drug-lovin' graduate of the freaky-fashion club-kid scene — a flamboyant homosexual who would wear foot-tall platform sneakers and plastic hot pants while spinning, sometimes dragging, around a nubile Puerto Rican slave teen on a studded leash. Even the Storm DJS adopted a schtick just to keep up: an apocalyptic doom act (to go with their hard-as-fuck techno style) taken to the But-is-it-irony? death-metal shattering point.

In 1993, Frankie Bones had a breakdown due to drug abuse. As his fall approached, his *Streetsound* columns became more and more venomous. Bones railed particularly against the status quo of the traditional American house scene. He got especially inflamed by the nauseatingly pious adulation classic house

DJ-producers like Frankie Knuckles or David Morales received from the ever-important British music press. "I'm sick of reading Euro dance mags that write corny profiles on all these producers who make so-so house. We *know* the house legends and the history. . . ."

Most British music critics and writers of note would never really get very excited about American rave. The culture came to North America too late to qualify on their trend-o-meter — long after the word *rave* had become dirtier than dirty to them. Frankie Bones's Storm Raves would start a domino effect in America, though. Throughout most of the nineties, rave would slowly spread through America, morphing as it went, settling into the different styles and different needs of the cities it touched.

2 SAN FRANCISCO
Peace, Love, Unity, and Utter Wickedness

The hottest gay club in San Francisco, 1978. The dance floor at the Trocadero superdisco is broiling. Thousands of shirtless men in gym shorts or jeans writhe into each other. Colored lights form a kaleidoscopic ceiling. Male go-go dancers wearing nothing but itty-bitty undies and work boots whirl like spinning tops over big black speakers, which are blaring out electronic hi-NRG disco: Sylvester's "You Make Me Feel (Mighty Real)," Boney M's "Daddy Cool."

The hottest gay club in San Francisco, 1988. The dance floor at the Colossus superdisco is broiling. Thousands of shirtless men in gym shorts or jeans writhe into each other. Male go-go dancers whirl like spinning tops over big black speakers, which are blaring out electronic hi-NRG disco: Frankie Goes to Hollywood's classic "Relax," Bad Boy Blue's "Come Back and Stay."

Two years after "the year house broke," San Francisco was still boogying to its traditional drummer. The gay clubs had not given up their favorite hi-NRG music for the new boom-boom of the Chicago jack. The gayest city in the United States didn't like house — too cold, too repetitive, not *gay* enough, were the general complaints. San Francisco's gay scene did not want to change. Pete Avila, a San Francisco gay DJ, remarks, "AIDS put a damper on the gay imagination for awhile. Especially in cities like San Francisco, where all the gay men pack themselves in together in the Castro [the city's gay ghetto]. The early-to-mid-eighties was not exactly a time for creative change for us. We suddenly had much bigger things to worry about. People wanted stability wherever they could find it."

There's a common myth in houseland that from 1986 on, house became *the* sound in all of America's gay clubs. It absolutely did not. In the eighties, hi-NRG music, a flashy, trashy, digi-disco — which began somewhere around Patrick Cowley's 1970s productions for Sylvester as well as Giorgio Morodor's work with Donna Summer, and then grew into the intense Europop-o-rama of Shannon, Frankie, and Hazell Dean in the 1980s at gay clubs like New York's the Saint — remained the favorite homo sound in much of the gay world. In many places, house came in a very distant second. "You can't underestimate the role AIDS played in the spreading problem house had in the US early on," says Avila. "Straights didn't want to touch anything gay, and many gays didn't want to touch anything experimental. At least not in San Fran."

Yet, in the late eighties, when the first wave of AIDS hysteria had cooled down, some DJs in San Francisco tried introducing the house sound. One of these DJs was Doc Martin, who started throwing a weekly club night called Recess. "Doc Martin was the first really important house DJ in San Francisco," says Dianna Jacobs — a Recess regular who eventually went on to promote large-scale raves called Toon Town. "He paved the way."

Doc, a huge man — probably about three hundred pounds huge — calls himself an "honorary fag." In 1987, when he was a doorman at San Francisco designer club the DNA Lounge, he took a trip to New York to visit the Paradise Garage before it closed. "When I came back to San Francisco, I was really turned on to house music. I was, like, 'We *need* this here.' Everything in San Francisco was so underdeveloped. The only place I knew of to buy house records was Tower Records at Fisherman's Wharf.

But they wouldn't let you listen to tracks first, and I didn't know any covers or producers — like, no magazines in the us were really writing about house, so I was shopping blindly, and it was impossible. I decided to try the gay stores — Butch Wax, the Record Track — in the Castro District. They had some of the music and were really intrigued by the fact that I actually wanted to play house. House wasn't a straight DJ thing in San Francisco. Actually, it wasn't really *anything* in San Francisco."

In February of 1989, Doc started Recess as a Saturday weekly at a three-hundred-capacity club called City Nights. His idea was to mix gays and straights together. "The idea was to make it crazy, different from other clubs — new music, new concepts!" he says. "The first night, I got a guy that rents roller skates at the Golden Gate Park to come into the club, and from 9 until 11:30 it was roller-skating for two bucks. I would play things like Ten City's 'That's the Way Love Is' and Black Box's 'Ride on Time.'" And I remember people's jaws would just drop when they walked into Recess. I'll never forget it — they didn't know *what* to do. Everyone, both gay and straight, was so used to, like, drink, dance, look cool, pick up, and go home — that was it. Gays did it in gay clubs, straights in straight clubs. But at Recess there was this drag queen in a mermaid's outfit in a swimming pool in the middle of the dance floor with apples around her in the water. And we promoted on both sides, so straight guys were, like, 'What the fuck is going on here!' Queers were, like, 'Whoa, there's too many straight people here!' Everyone was confused. But I thought, 'No, this is what it should be about. Everyone together.' It's so San Francisco a thing, isn't it?"

Doc Martin canned the night when it hit a plateau after only six weeks. After the novelty had worn off, his crowd just stopped coming. He soon moved to Los Angeles, drawn to that city's more developed house scene and unfolding rave culture. Subsequently, he became a favorite DJ on the American rave circuit and, later still, a regular at British house clubs like Ministry of Sound.

Pete Avila, then playing commercial Europop at a club called DV8, was impressed by Doc Martin's "crazy" idea of house music and gay/straight mixing at Recess. And, as Martin had before him, Avila returned home to San Francisco after visiting New York with a mission "to make things happen."

"It was in 1989, and I was getting friendly with the owner of DV8, this old, eccentric San Francisco freak named Doctor Winkie," says Avila. "Winkie was in the process of evicting people from the third floor of DV8's building — which was office space, all these different rooms. I talked him into fixing that whole space up. He ended up calling the space the Pleasure Zone. It was part of his whole empire. He also had a restaurant called the Caribbean Zone. Everything was a zone. Winkie was the right man for this idea, though. I mean, this guy soon commissioned Keith Haring to come out and paint these murals on the walls of the Pleasure Zone. And before Keith Haring arrived, Winkie pulled a fast one and arranged to have canvasses stretched the size of the walls. Now, Keith was coming in thinking that he would just paint regular wall murals — you know, like, zip, zap, graffiti fast. And when he got here, he was, like, 'No way. I am not painting these huge paintings. Nice try.' So Winkie supplied him with a bunch of cocaine and said, 'Here, you can have my Mercedes, too.' Keith Haring ended up painting the canvasses."

Doctor Winkie gave Avila Thursday nights to handle as he pleased. Avila called his night Osmosis. The night was only mildly successful, but it was instrumental in gathering a group of people together who would go on to form the nucleus of San Francisco's rave movement. "Osmosis was one of the first clubs outside the gay scene proper where you could get Ecstasy," Avila explains. "People were starting to read about the Ecstasy thing [that was happening] in England, and they were curious. I guess the club had a bit of an E vibe. We got fog machines, so it was always foggy. There was a lot of freakiness going on, too. There were these bedrooms where you could shut doors and actually go in and be alone."

Avila continues: "Osmosis was happening at the same time as when this group of English kids were moving to San Francisco. About half a dozen English kids. They were all into this acid-house thing. And they all DJed. I was the one who gave them their first [DJing] sets in this city. I used to mix the warm stuff, like Alias's [deep-house anthem] 'Follow Me,' and then let them play their acid, techno stuff — 'Cubik' by 808 State, all that English less-soulful stuff. They didn't quite fit, but they were so *eager*. I wanted to give them a chance, you know?"

◆

This is the point, San Franciscans will tell you, at which the "Brits invaded." Or, "the British conquered." Or, "the British Mafia took over." It is also the point at which house music and rave culture really jetted off in San Fran and began morphing into new, not-New-York-at-all shapes — shapes more het than homo. The "English group" Pete Avila had given a break to at Osmosis — DJs Jenö, Garth, and Markie Mark — soon formed what they called a "dance collective." They named themselves Wicked, and decided, with their friend Alan McQueen — who, back in London, had promoted acid nights at the Brain Club — to throw parties of their own. Free parties on beaches — full-moon parties.

All the members of the Wicked collective were either followers of, or active participants in, a British acid-house sound system called Tonka, one of the movable-speaker armies that flourished during England's acid epiphany of the late 1980s. Tonka's granddad was an old Cambridge head named Robert, who, legend has it, bought Pink Floyd's speaker stack in the late 1960s so he could do parties on England's hippie free-festival circuit. Robert was a smack addict and a capital-C Character. He had handlebar moustaches and red, green, and gold false teeth.

He assembled LSD parties that would start out in a squatted venue, continue on rented double-decker buses, and end on a beach. At which point, things would often be moving towards the psycho side of psychedelic.

In the eighties, Robert teamed his system up with a bunch of hip-hop and dub DJs who were trying to scratch mix, and they called themselves TDK — the Tone Def Kru. As acid house swept England, TDK painted its speakers bright yellow and renamed itself Tonka. Made up of DJs Harvey, Choci, Markie Mark, Thomas, and Rev, Tonka became known as an "alternative" house collective. It operated outside the world of big-city clubs and sly-guy rave promoters "in it for the money." This collective had a wishful anarchist/spiritualist agenda, and it threw free parties in the wilds and on beaches, in school halls and in squats (funded by monthly pay parties held at Brighton's Zap! Club). Along with other companies, like Nottingham's DiY or Liverpool's Bass Evangelists, Tonka was a crucial element in a scene that by the 1990 Glastonbury Festival had created the altogether surprising combination of crusty travelers in horse-drawn carriages, Mohawked squatters, and the latest techno and house records.

The Wickeds-to-be left England one by one throughout 1990. Garth went to San Francisco on a whim, told Markie to visit, and so on; each helped the other out with airplane tickets and places to stay. "We were leaving England," recalls Jenö, "because things were just crumbling there. Once one of us arrived in San Francisco, we'd call back home and be, like, 'You *have* to get over here! The sun is shining, there are no problems, it's so laid back! Like, sell my car, buy a plane ticket with the money, and just *come*!" Jenö also says that the crew wanted out of England because "rave was just getting too big and too disgusting and too commercial." The early-nineties ascendancy of hardcore, megaraves and money-minded promoters went against the conscious, politicized nature of the techno-hippie rave stream in which Tonka was ensconced. At the same time, the roving Tonka lifestyle was being actively paralyzed in England. It was criminalized by conservative politicians, brutalized by police, and blacklisted by landowners; the culmination of this process would take the form of the British government's impossibly convoluted 1994 Criminal Justice Bill, designed to make the lifestyles of the nonsettled practically illegal: New Age travelers, ravers, eco-warriors, and squatters became "problem" factions. Scum in need of suppression.

San Francisco kids were magnetically drawn to Wicked and its counterculture rave ideologies, its stories of peace parties and one-love, open-air free raves and mind-expanding drugs. The idea of dancing for enlightenment rather than sheer carnal pleasure ("simple hedonism" or "going out to get laid") appealed to San Francisco's youth sector, which is primarily made up of people born elsewhere, many of whom moved to the Bay Area to find enlightenment or acceptance. Maybe the kids drawn to Wicked were seeking a bit of meaning within the fat, myth-filled chasm the hippie boom of the sixties had opened. And maybe the answer was to be found in this English rave thing.

"People were very accepting and I guess you could say naïve," says Jenö. "San Francisco is like a city full of searching people. And because out here, you know, 'European is cool,' people were interested in the things that we had grown up around — really basic things. We were admired for being English. Like White people arriving in Africa, and their whiteness meaning they are received as gods. That interest in us allowed us to set down our own blueprint for what became rave in San Francisco. We were, like, 'OK, we don't have much to go on here, but what we do have is what we know worked in England.' We took the acid-house smiley face and had whistles, strobe lights and stuff at the first parties — you know, things we would never have done in England at that time. We definitely hooked into what had been new in England years before but had never arrived here. Then we defined it. Of course, in San Francisco the end result was nothing like what it was in England. The attitude is too different. But we introduced people to those elements — the same elements that ran through the whole house culture from the Paradise Garage to the rave thing: a lot of respect for each other and love . . . you know, those kind of young, idealistic ideals. People here liked that."

Wicked's Full Moon parties are the most defining bit of San Francisco's rave history. These raves quickly took on the unreal feel of a pagan ritual set to the very strong Ecstasy and LSD available in the Bay Area — something like a housey cousin to the Burning Man Festival, the hippie gathering that happens annually in Nevada's Black Rock Desert. Wicked had annexed a new crowd, a predominantly straight, White crowd, many members of which were experiencing a dance-music scene for the very first time: Deadheads, folkies, students whose walls were plastered with Jane's Addiction posters.

"The first parties that really got my attention and made me want to come [to San Francisco] and spend some serious time here was the Full Moons. And I was not the only one — the parties were very appealing," says Wade Hampton, a self-described "rich kid" from Texas who was instrumental in setting up rave scenes in places as diverse as Los Angeles and Chicago and now owns a record shop in San Francisco. "Wicked had somehow tapered the British rave thing to appeal to a very San Francisco sensibility. There was no Vick's Vaporub. More like tie-dye, people and their dogs, and mystical feelings circulating."

The collective, soon joined by another ex-Tonka DJ, Thomas, raised money for the Full Moon raves with a weekly night in the basement of a Thai restaurant. This dank space had an aged cabaret license, and the Thai restaurant owners had given it the neon-worthy name Big Heart City and called it a club. Before Wicked, Big Heart City was most often used by local Goth bands or heavy-metal promoters. "We started a Friday-nighter there, just called Wicked, and we all DJd there," says Garth. "We did a little flyer. There was a smiley on it. And on the back, we had a quote from Tim Leary — um, something about the group experience or dancing or something." Wicked's Friday packed the place solid. People were lining up outside, blowing their whistles on the street. "It kinda reminded me of the famous scenes from England at the dawn of acid house when parties would erupt on streets after the clubs closed." But when the parties hit the beaches, continues Garth, "we stopped being so concerned with our memories from back home and started understanding the magnitude of what we could do in the fantastic city we were in."

The first Full Moon Rave was in March of 1991. "It was totally bare bones," recalls Garth. "We had become friends with this San Francisco DJ, Ernie Munsen, and he had a truck. We shoved a sound system in and drove out to Baker Beach. We just kinda told people — you know, word of mouth. About eighty showed: eighty really key people. It was a beautiful morning, like the fog was rolling back over the Golden Gate Bridge, and we were all blown away that we'd actually done this. That we were in San Francisco and we were having a proper acid-house party. We couldn't believe it."

So the collective did these parties every month. At the first anniversary of the Full Moon Raves, there were a thousand people dancing on a Santa Cruz beach. By the third anniversary, there were three thousand dancing at Bonnie Dune without a promotional flyer in sight. Wicked had used the "telephone tree" technique: they called a handful of "key people" the night of the rave and those people each called a few more people, and so on, and so on. "The parties were consistent; they would just get bigger every time," says Jenö. "It didn't matter if it was raining, snowing, freezing, sunny — they just got bigger, friends bringing friends. And people would wait really late. We would get to the beaches at, like, 2 A.M., and it would take us a long time to set up the system. But people would just sit in their cars, waiting until the music started."

More than that of any of the other Wicked DJs, Jenö's DJing has left its mark on San Francisco's dance scene. In the era of the Full Moons, Jenö was unquestionably seen as a shaman (not just a DJ), and the reverence for his "extrasensory" powers lives on in the city's postrave enclave. "He could take you to outer space," says Toon Town's Dianna Jacobs. "His music was *sooo* trippy. Jenö had this ability to do spatial things. One night, I went up to him and was just, like, 'You are an alien. I've seen your space ship. You are from another planet.' We had never heard music played like that before."

By about 1991, Jenö had caught on to English records like those bearing the Shut Up and Dance label, records that relied on the syncopated breakbeat rhythm associated with funk and hip-hop — not the 4/4 beat more standard in American house. He fixed these early breakbeats (which, in the UK, would morph into the sound of hardcore and, later, jungle) to a fly American funk, to the loopy mellow-yellowness and acid-rock heritage of San Francisco itself, and to his own genuine love for the 303 acid squelch, instrumental house, and ambient sounds. The result was something of a trippy-housey acid funk, a style that would be picked up by innumerable San Francisco DJs and producers in years to come and, by 1994, earn itself the tag "San Frandisco." "This was the rave scene's total cutaway," says Dianna Jacobs. "Because before Jenö, all San Fran had was, like, Pete Avila and [his] gay bent — mostly diva house, deep house."

"Jenö's breaks were supergroovy and psychedelic," explains Doc Martin, "and his mixing was so smooth. It's weird: all the San Francisco DJs were expecting him to play all this thumpy acid house because an early tape that he made [called *We Are Phuture*] had been circulating, and that's what was on it. So when he started this breakbeat business, he threw us all. Everyone loved his sound. It was perfect for beaches."

For many of the Full Moon patrons, the parties started taking on rather mystical meanings. Punters began to use terms like

"tribal ritual" a lot, and they experimented not only with Ecstasy, but also with a plethora of strong psychedelic drugs (like DMT). "People were trying to fashion these beach parties into much more than just parties," says Wade Hampton — more like cosmic coincidences between people, a sound system, a beach, and a big, round moon. "People were getting pretty mental with, like hippie-shit natural[ism] and cosmic stuff," continues Hampton. "All kinds of freaky things started getting really popular. There was a kind of one-upmanship going on [in] the crowd. I remember at one party, after a night that lasted like twelve hours, sitting out on this rock in the middle of the beach — a rock that looked like the Prudential rock, this stark thing sitting in the middle of this sandy bay. I could see from one side of the cliff line all the way to the other, and in every single direction there was something amazing going on. People hang gliding, or two hundred people nude on the beach, people on stilts, people on unicycles, every Northern California weirdo thing you could imagine, filling the sky and the beach for miles. There were just so many people involved here, bringing in their two cents. In a way, I guess typical rave stuff — like whistles and face masks — is also bringing your two cents, too, but this was different. This was really back-to-Mother-Earth California stuff."

This Mother Earth connection at the Full Moons soon starting warping into ideas about universal connections. "I saw the same aliens as, like, two hundred people at one Full Moon, and I am not exactly a superhuge believer in that sort of thing," admits Hampton. "But, I'm telling you right now, that shit came in . . . so many people saw the same things as I did. The parties were, well, they were making magic."

"Magic, yes," agrees Jason Walker, an expat Brit, who occasionally helped Wicked schlep speakers up and down the sand dunes. "I remember one Full Moon at Grey Whale Cove, down on Santa Cruz Beach — the most beautiful, magical place I had ever seen. People as far as the eye could see. As everyone started coming up on their Ecstasy and their psychedelics, a huge ring formed around the DJ booth. Everybody holding hands and spinning, running in a fast circle. To me, it was like going back to witchcraft or something — pagan magic rituals. It was so out of hand, like we were tapping into something [that was] just taking us in these directions. Nobody was sitting around brewing up these tricks. Fuck! The music just made you do it. It was the chemistry of everything. You couldn't help but think, 'Wow. We're linking up with some cosmic things here; this is awesome . . . if there was only some way we could put this power towards benefiting mankind.'"

Walker would soon befriend Malachy O'Brien — newly arrived from County Tyrone, Northern Ireland — and the pair would try to do exactly that. They created a weekly club night, at a club called 1015 Folsom, entitled Come-Unity, a "thinking-person's club night" that was a neat complement to the uni-cycles, flowing hedonism, and developing rave theories of the Wicked events. They would also begin throwing occasional raves with another Irishman, named Martin O'Brien (no relation to Malachy), under the title the Gathering. "Our idea was not nec-essarily musical, like Wicked's, but more cultural," says Walker. "Like, 'Rave is changing consciousness as a generation. Hope-fully, we can do something with it [and] not be left in the dust like lots of the sixties folks.' To do that, it needed more informa-tion-giving, more than what Wicked was doing."

Everything at Come-Unity *meant* something. The name of the club night itself, says Malachy, was "from us asking unity to be our friend . . . like, 'Come, Unity.' We were calling it." They gave out pamphlets and flyers at their parties containing bits and bobs taken from neohippie publications, rave zines, and English folk psychedelia. "A bit of consciousness, really," remarks Malachy. "You know, the power of the group collective, a lot of planetary ecological stuff. We wanted to teach people to live more holistically." Come-Unity referenced San Francisco's sixties cultural heyday quite liberally. "What happened in England in the 1980s, with the Summer of Love, is essentially what happened here in the 1960s in the Summer of Love," says Malachy. "In the 1960s, something happened to people on LSD, and they wanted others to share it. It was the same with Ecstasy. Something was trying to expand our consciousness. The same kind of movement." Malachy and company often bolstered their own retro-isms with Xeroxed snatches of the "zippie" writings of Fraser Clarke (the Scottish creator of *Encyclopaedia Psychedelia* and *Evolution* magazines, who believed that rave was a rebirth of the hippie movement, not to mention a rebirth of "ancient shamanic rituals," a way of using technology for the good of the enlightened individual rather than the good of meanie society).

Soon punters started coming in with their own homemade-theory flyers. Quasi-religious writings titled "Cybertribe Rising" and "House Music=Horizontal Communication=Healthy Planet" circulated. Desperate calls were issued to "dance the design of a new civilization," to follow "Britain's first communal altered state since Sgt. Pepper," to "stop rave from becoming a passive hedonistic trend," to "hook up with the cosmologic program," to "say no to . . . the sad inmates of Modern Society" and to those who "just want us to have fun." "Maybe we don't think too much about what we're doing," reads one flyer written by someone named C.T., "cuz then we might realize that we've stumbled onto the Secret of the Ages, and actually start doing something with it."

In this insanely hyperbolic mash of paganism and futurism, America and Amerika, the sixties and prehistory, cyber whatnot and green living, promoters were emerging not as party makers but as "spiritual leaders," just as DJs like Jenö were no longer entertainers, or even artists, but shamans. People were being built up as gurus 'n gods, and Malachy, with his sincere desire to better mankind and his soft, sweet demeanor, was in the premier league of these new gods. "Malachy? He was the man! The Man!

He was the spiritual leader — know what I mean?" exalts the Gathering's Martin O'Brien. "He showed me the light. Took me by the hand and showed it to me. He doesn't even know he's done it. For awhile there, he got everyone working together. He had a power."

◆

Another person who was graced with this kind of leader status was yet another Briton: a Londoner in his twenties named Mark Heley, who arrived in San Francisco in 1991. Heley moved in with Dianna Jacobs, former collegiate soccer champ and Osmosis graduate. At the time, Jacobs was putting on small, more clubby events with partner Preston Lytton. "Kinda androgynous, keeping the Osmosis flame alive," she explains. "Our trip was more club-kiddy — like, glittery, glammy . . . we threw parties with names like Stacey's Seafood Salad, and everybody got dressed up. Mark Heley thought it was all rather infantile, and I was sold on anything he said, so I started thinking so, too. When I first met him, I was, like, 'Oooh! Big words! A philosophy degree from Cambridge!' He was so incredibly opinionated, he had so many ideas about all this rave stuff, he scared me so much I fell hopelessly in love with him and asked him to join in on our parties."

In England, Heley had been a journalist. He'd written about rave culture for British style bibles *i-D* and *The Face*; he had also contributed to Fraser Clarke's *Evolution* and Silicon Valley "mindstyle" fringe zine *Mondo 2000*. To San Francisco's growing population of rave kids, his credentials could not have been more smasheroo. "He was the instant Billy Graham of the rave scene," says 1015 Folsom owner Ira Sandler, "before he even did anything."

Preston Lytton, Dianna Jacobs, and Mark Heley called their new promotions company Toon Town. Their first party took place in a warehouse on Federal Street in the spring of 1992.

"Me and Preston found the space," says Jacobs. "Mark Heley came up with all the ideas." The Come-Unity crew had already introduced texts that joined Silicon Valley and Haight-Ashbury, but Come-Unity's setup — banners, electric lights, two turntables, Xerox flyers — was not exactly a cyberama. Heley wanted his techno-spiritual ideas to be visibly active. He decided on the theme of a "technology playground" for the first Toon Town, borrowing virtual-reality systems and lasers and all kinds of compu-gadgets from his friends at *Mondo 2000*, friends who became the rave's coproducers. Heley also introduced "smart drugs" into the San Fran rave mix — pills and drinks concocted of amino acids, nutrients, or recontextualized medicines like anticonvulsants that supposedly stimulated everything from short-term memory to concentration. The kind of glossy Technicolor cartoony flyers and ferociously organized mass distribution that Wicked had shied away from, Heley insisted upon.

Fifteen hundred kids came to Toon Town's rave. "It was obvious," says Jenö, who was DJing at the party, "that this was a second wave of San Francisco raving. The crowd was much more teen than ours." Dancers went to Wickeds with whistles. They left Come-Unity with jargony awareness pamphlets. But they arrived at Toon Town wearing floppy pom-pom hats and long-sleeved T-shirts printed with glow-in-the-dark patterns that would trip on strobes. They wore face masks with Vick's Vaporub slathered inside, just like the British hardcore ravers. They sported ski goggles, tie-dyed clothing, smiley amulets on toilet chains, alien logos, Terminator sunglasses, electrical-wiring accessories, and shoes spray-painted silver. They dressed for a DIY future. They drank fluorescent smart drinks. They tried VR systems and Brain Machines. And when they left Toon Town — still buzzing on a multimedia high, quite ready for a psychedelic apocalypse — they left as capital-R Ravers. "As in Rave is something you are," says Jacobs, "not only something you do." This was a far cry from hazily tripping on sunshine.

"The idea," continues Jacobs, "was very clear and very Mark Heley and very successful. Our parties were to be a place where people could come and experience technology in a different setting, which would allow them to think differently about it and devise new uses for it. It was embracing technology and cyberculture not as the enemy but as a way to create community. A road to a new peace. Taking technology out of its capitalist context. Mark Heley introduced the *Mondo 2000* people into the thing. The club kids started reading *Mondo* and talked to these *Mondo* people, who seemed so fabulous. It was, like, all those people with all of their different experiences coming together and *thinking*! Obviously, we pushed the smart-drug thing very hard, as a complement."

In 1992, Heley told the *San Francisco Examiner* that "In England . . . people are very phobic about touching and Ecstasy gave them a tremendous release." Being touchy-feely is not exactly a problem in San Francisco, but "thinking drugs" were attractive. "It was mind expansion, like the sixties, only with nineties drugs," says Jacobs. Still, this wasn't "tune in, turn on, and drop out." It was "tune in, tune in, and tune in." A woman who'd dubbed herself "Earth Girl" started a smart-drink company, selling products with such names as Energy Elicksure and Psuper Psonic Psyber Tonic. "But it was just a smokescreen," declares Ira Sandler, "because the real drug of the Toon Town scene was E, and everybody knew that. The people selling the smart drinks and stuff would do it on the pitch that 'this stuff makes your E work better.' And I don't think it's a coincidence that Mark Heley had been selling the smart stuff back in England. Things started feeling a bit hoaxy, and kids kinda knew that, but they still bought the smart baloney."

But, smokescreen or no, the combination of good-guy technology, smart-drug hype, real-drug euphoria, house music, and *thinking* was incendiary. By the time Toon Town's 1992–93 New Year's party had happened, in a seven-thousand-capacity room in a shopping mall, rave had become a real honeytrap in San Francisco. There were now two strands: first there was the Wicked/Come-Unity side, which associated itself with the past (that is, the 1960s, England's acid 1980s, prehistory); then there was a second wave, a younger crowd turned on by Toon Town's over-the-top future schlock and expensive design. "Mark Heley may have had all kinds of talk," says Sandler, "but what he really ended up showing was that in order for rave to succeed broadly, it needed to be as concretely capitalist as it was ephemeral. And the older school, the Full Moon sensualists, hated that."

Rave was bulking up into a full-blown leisure industry in San Francisco. The Upper Haight became the daytime meeting place, and Toon Towny rave kids became the area's visible majority. The weirdo dress sense of the first Toon Towners had homogenized into what was becoming the set of North American rave essentials: extremely small kid's clothing mixed with extremely large styles nicked from skate-boarding and hip-hop cultures, plus such ubiquitous Ameri-rave accessories as pocket wallets with long, thick chains looped up to army click belts, woolly hats with bubbly fonted logo patches, wraparound specs, 1970s track suits, *Sesame Street* paraphernalia, children's backpacks, beaded jewelry, old-school sneakers with oversized laces. Peace-pin souvenir shops on the Haight were being taken over by stores like HouseWares and Ameba — San Francisco's rave centrals — which sold clothing, stickers, zines, and mix tapes. These establishments also distributed rave tickets and flyers for upcoming events. A graphic designer named Nick Philip created a San Fran rave-gear company called Anarchic Adjustment, specializing in T-shirts emblazoned with buzz phrases like "open your mind" and images of aliens; the company was soon raking in thirty thousand dollars a season. And dozens of rave-promotion companies were popping up through the ecstatic ether. "By 1993," says Sandler, "literally any doorman, any slide-projector guy, any flyer person, light man, busboy, had their own party coming up. Everyone became promoters. Ravers throwing raves. Everyone wanted fame and money. It was this weird pinnacle."

Toon Town was driven to make its New Year's Eve bash — an extravaganza to be held in the Expo Hall of the Fashion Center on Townsend Street — the biggest rave San Fran had ever seen. Preston Lytton had left the trio "because he didn't get along with Mark Heley," says Jacobs, and so new partners — "business types" — were brought in. The party was in the planning stages a full six months. Ads were placed in all the alternative weeklies and a three-page press release was sent out. The party was called Psychedelic Apocalypse, a "theme park for your brain." "Counseling information," promised the press release, written by Heley, "will be made available to those unable to return to 'reality.'" One hundred thousand dollars was invested in the undertaking. "We felt like we needed a large amount of stuff," explains Jacobs. Heley's press release details this "stuff," and here, quoted directly, is only about half of it:

Points of Interest:
- The Holographic Exploratorium
  An 8,000 square foot exhibition featuring more than 40 installations
- Around-the-World Videophone Link
  Midnight celebration from New York (9 P.M.) and Hawaii (2 P.M.)
- Virtual Reality
  Experience the Toon Town Virtual World by the Renaissance Foundation
- 3-D Video
  A giant screen system with headsets for 16 people
- Mandala system multimedia
  Step into a giant screen video on this virtual video system
- Video toaster/Fairlight interactive video

- Computer animation/'scratch' video from Tokyo's Hyper-delic
- Neurotechnology by Inner Technologies
- Installations by Digital Media and Anarchic Adjustment
- Smart Bar by The Nutrient Café
  Featuring the world premiere of two completely new smart drinks and smart ice cream!
- Three state-of-the-art laser installations
- Giant psychedelic lightshow on five screens by Look/See Visuals and Fly by Light
- Intelligent lighting by Impact lighting

The party lured an astonishing number of people. By then, Heley had already successfully assimilated the *Mondo 2000* group into the Toon Town zone, and the magazine became quote fodder for newbie ravers. *Mondo 2000* is quite a high-talking magazine. Heley's initial advice to ravers that they should rethink technology into a groovy friend had given rise to one terribly complicated disseminator; *Mondo* was filled with new-edge cyberspeak, interviews with deified drug gurus, pretentious fancy-danciness about fractals and virtual whatnot and smart chemicals and techno-animism and trance states and conspiracy theories. "I felt like all the cybershtick was getting a bit out of hand," says Jacobs. "Like, at this point, it was mainly teens at our parties. I'm not sure if Mark Heley's message was necessarily penetrating and if this big, complicated message wasn't, like, turning into his own power-trippy thing. Like, you are eighteen. You hear all this *Mondo* talk at a rave, on E. What do you *do* with it? Try to figure out what it means? I didn't even know, and I was one of the goddamned promoters!"

"Something turned sour after that party," says Sandler. "Heley started seeming like this renegade tyrant, a power maniac. He made DJs sign exclusivity deals — even light men had to, and graphic designers. And, for a very defining six to seven months, he was the power person over all other promoters, which cast a bit of a dark vibe over things." After Psychedelic Apocalypse (which took in $175,000), Jacobs and Heley, who had become romantically involved, broke up. "I was living on this tiny salary. I had given away all the power," says Jacobs. "There were all these investors and people, and they would never give me the facts. Heley would yell at me when I asked about it." Jacobs was sleeping in the Toon Town office by the time she took her partners to court. By the time she dropped the case ("emotional stress"), she says, "it was kinda known among San Francisco DJs and promoters that Mark Heley had become a pretty ugly character. Everything was fragmenting. At this point it was, like, 'Unity, my ass!' It was all sort of going downhill."

In his history of rave culture, *Energy Flash*, Simon Reynolds points out that "any given rave scene seems to enjoy a honeymoon period of two years, tops, before problems begin to appear." The crumbling of the San Francisco rave scene — the fall of Toon Town, the annulment of the Full Moons in 1994, and the pushing out of all one-off parties into the suburbs, established nightclubs, or oblivion — was the product of both internal developments (like infighting, greediness, mass drug burnout) and external forces (like the police).

San Francisco's rave environment had been undisturbed by police intervention until 1993, when the force began to crack down on non-city-sanctioned one-offs. "It had real Catholic overtones to it," says Sandler. "There was a Catholic mayor, a Catholic chief of police; there were a lot of people who felt that this city was way too permissive and that it needed to go in the opposite direction. Promoters were getting sucker punched left and right. [City Hall] had police who were very good at infiltration. They caught on to all the phone lines, they would check every single flyer, they would, like, float from one roof to another. They had narcs in with ravers. The police took this really seriously."

The necessary permits became impossible to obtain in San Francisco. For a short period, the odd promoter would get away with throwing a party by employing a Frankie Bones-style crafty deception: hiring a camera or two and claiming to be doing a video shoot; or declaring that two thousand gurning kids in a warehouse were actually guests at a wedding and staging a faux ceremony in the middle of the rave to prove it.

But tactics like these can only be effective once or twice. The Gathering's Martin O'Brien, who still throws raves in the Bay Area, was among the first to move his parties out of San Francisco proper and into the suburbs. "Even by the first Toon Town — like, April 1992 — the police were onto it. I knew that, so I did raves all over the fucking place: Valejo, Oakland, all over the East Bay. We broke into warehouses in Union City — fucking madcap — just took 'em over and the cops wouldn't do anything about it. They weren't onto all this outside of San Francisco. It was cool, but it probably did do something to decentralize the scene. Many San Francisco promoters started doing all-night raves in nightclubs instead."

San Francisco City Hall had its trump card ready, though: a disused law, to be used "as an emergency measure," one that would affect a good proportion of the ravers in the city because it applied to teenagers. "In 1974," says O'Brien, "California State law lowered the age of a minor to eighteen. But in 1993, San Francisco still had, apparently, a law on its books that said you are a minor if you're under twenty-one. And there was a statement in the cabaret law that said 'No minor shall enter a cabaret establishment between the hours of 2 and 6 A.M.' So, all of a sudden, they unearthed this bullshit law. I mean, they didn't stop people from *voting* if they were under twenty-one! And they would go in, raid all these nightclubs . . . pull everyone out, and ask for ID. A bunch of us got together and made slogan

T-shirts, got a lawyer, and took it to court. And it got thrown out of court."

In most cities where the police have gone strong-arm on rave, you will encounter the same urban myth: The chief of police's daughter. Goes to a rave. Comes home stoned. Daddy makes it his personal mission to thwart the bad influence. In the case of San Francisco, the dad was a sergeant, and his name was Bouchard. The rave his daughter went to was a Wicked event. "Sergeant Bouchard — bastard! — he had this vendetta against us, against Alan [McQueen] in particular," says Wicked's Markie Mark. "Alan was the face at the front of Wicked at the time — like, he was the promoter. Bouchard had it in for Alan — arrested him for all sorts, arrested him for having a pipe in his pocket once."

The Full Moons, which had vibed through 1991 and most of 1992 with very little police intervention, became, in 1993, the police symbol for the "rave problem." So, by the fall, Wicked had also moved their parties outside the San Francisco city limits; they usually happened at a Santa Cruz beach called Bonnie Dune, a kind of jumbo natural fortress bunkered by miles of beach, dunes, and cliffs. "We never had one shut down at Bonnie Dune," says Markie Mark. "They'd need such a large force. They'd have to climb over the dunes and down onto the beach. It was a quarter of a mile into the darkness away from anywhere you could park your car."

Despite this natural protection from the police, the scene at Bonnie Dune was still, according to Jenö, "going downhill on its own. It was getting uncontrollable. There were too many people. Too many drugs. I remember one time, I was playing records, right, and everyone is dancing. I look down to change the record, look up, and no one is dancing. I was, like, 'Oh, what? Bad track?' No! There was this guy who had fallen off the cliff and literally landed on his head. He stood up, wobbled about a bit, and then he was fine and went off. The following month, this other guy — I guess he was having such a great time that he thought he was a dolphin or something — jumped off the cliffs into the water. You should see these cliffs: they are high, jagged, with very difficult waters underneath and waves and rocks and stuff. Then another man jumped in a fire nude, all freaked out on drugs, and he had to be dragged out. Somebody called an ambulance, but we were so far from any hospital, so a medical helicopter was sent instead. But they couldn't land it anywhere. They tried to land it on the road, but all the cars were getting [in the way]. So they had to send the helicopter back. It didn't stop the party, but we were freaked. We were, like, 'OK, we're getting to that point where things like this happen.' It was a precursor. I can see it now. It was a buildup to what would happen."

At the March 1993 Full Moon, the sensation at Bonnie Dune was particularly ecstatic. "Something about that one," says Markie Mark. "There was a real sense of community. It was really strong — stronger than usual, it seemed." After the party, once the sound system had been packed into the Wicked van, Alan McQueen, his girlfriend, Trish, and Come-Unity's Malachy O'Brien shared a joint and decided to head into Santa Cruz with a couple of friends before going home. "We wanted to get some coffee and donuts at this place called the Flying Saucer," says Malachy. "Alan was driving the van, a rickety old thing. I was in the back with my dog and all the speakers. I think Alan had done a bit of acid that night. He fell asleep and lost control of the vehicle at Candlestick Park — ironically, a location of one of the earlier Full Moons. There was a very amusing piece of art there. It was called *A Drum Set for Future Primitives*. I loved it. It was all galvanized metal columns, sheared off, a big crude metal thing coming out of the earth. . . . I'll never forget that."

The van careened into the bay, but the tide was out so it landed and rolled over in the mud — "a big crude metal thing coming out of the earth." Everyone who had been riding in the front got out fine, but Malachy, in the back, was crushed under the sound system. He was permanently paralyzed from the neck down.

After Malachy's accident, everything in San Francisco changed. The Wickeds stopped promoting Full Moon parties and concentrated on DJing out of town. Toon Town was no more. Alan McQueen and Trish got deported. "It made a lot of people, a lot of the kids, stop and think," says Sandler. "Like, *he* said, 'Embracing smart drugs and technology will lead you. . . .' *It didn't. They* said, 'Computers are going to lead you. . . .' *They didn't,* 'Dancing outside is going to lead you. . . .' *It didn't.* All these messages: 'We're at the golden age! Nirvana!' . . . But it just wasn't. *It wasn't.* It never got there." Yet, no matter how fractured and disillusioned the scene became, Malachy's tragic accident had somehow galvanized San Francisco's original wish for a scene based on unity and love. The rave promoters in the Bay Area — every single one of them — joined together to throw a benefit rave for Malachy.

"Many people saw Malachy as this spiritual leader," says Markie Mark. "Or they wanted him to be that. I think when a lot of psychedelics and drugs are going down, people's extrasensory wishes kind of . . . well . . . people start looking for more. But these were people looking for leadership in someone else when they couldn't find it in themselves. And that used to freak me out about the raves. There were a lot of people just lost. And the energy and what was going on at the beginning was wonderful. But people didn't feed it back into their lives. They gave up their lives and were, like, 'I want to live the rave.' And, eventually, many became full-time partyers, so they had no experience to feed back into the scene. The Malachy event sparked this sense of purpose. People were trying to tack this almost religious significance on it, like, 'It's a sign.'"

Bay Area promoters and DJs came together for some "extremely torrid" meetings, organized by Martin O'Brien. It was decided that the benefit should be called Unity. The party began with a blessing by a Buddhist monk and ended with a live video feed of Malachy from his hospital bed; it raised one hundred thousand dollars, which enabled Malachy to return to the UK for rehabilitation. True to form, he gave much of the leftover money to charity. "In the strangest way, the party was what I had always dreamed of," says Malachy, who still throws Come-Unities irregularly (but his remaining financial support comes from Martin O'Brien). "Like, the unity Come-Unity was calling had finally arrived. I was glad, you see? The next day my finger had moved. It hadn't moved before. And it hasn't moved since. But some days I do feel things. I'll have some sensation in my feet. I can still go out and dance in my imagination. Dance with other people by putting my head in their feet. So I really feel like there is hope. Nothing is ever in vain. You know — action, reaction."

✦

After Malachy's accident, Wicked was scapegoated. "Fucking Brits!" says San Francisco house producer Scott Hardkiss. "They come over here with records that were made in *America* five years before they came and they say they are ambassadors for house culture — like, it wouldn't have happened if they didn't come . . . and then they do their things and leave everything a mess!" It was as if any twinge that San Francisco scensters may have felt about the English coming in and setting up camp had mushroomed into jealousy and hatred after the tragedy. People needed to blame someone. Some blamed Wicked for the intrinsic failure of a youth movement gone bonkers on inflated hopes. Rave did not rainbow-swoop all these searching people back to Eden. As Ira Sandler says, "It *didn't.*"

By 1994, the very word *rave* had become stigmatized. Sunshine Jones of the San Francisco hippie-house outfit Dubtribe began writing a column under the pen name Fabio Jones ("a gay Black man from Saskatchewan" — Sunshine is a straight, White San Franciscan) for house-culture magazine *XLR8R*. In his column, Sunshine/Fabio was prone to slamming "a dark and evil force . . . those Wicked wankers." "Rave over, baby," he wrote in one edition; "time to move on." Dubtribe was part of a move to "Americanize" the San Francisco party scene. "House music is a national treasure, a national, spiritual treasure," Sunshine proclaimed. "I don't know why this city needed British people to educate them on something that was born here."

The active undercutting of the British was also being pursued by another group of San Francisco house producers called the Hardkiss Brothers. The Hardkisses — Scott Friedel, Robbie Cameron, and Gavin Bieber — had a master plan from the day they landed in San Fran after finishing college, at the start of Full Moon mania. "We wanted to be like great American rock stars," deadpans Scott Hardkiss. They tried throwing parties advertised with flyers spoofing the Wicked schtick (Wicked had a flyer that read, "Only for the headstrong"; the Hardkisses made one that read, "Good morning Bay Area, this is your wake-up call" and then "only for the *heart*strong"). "The reaction was painful," says Robbie Hardkiss. "People had gotten used to this kind of British subtlety. But to us, it seemed like laziness. Like, we were raised in America [although Gavin Bieber was born in South Africa] and we are proud of who we are and we felt totally comfortable shouting about it."

"The British Mafia couldn't handle it," says Scott Hardkiss. "They trashed us. Don't let people tell you about Full Moon spirituality. It was a mask! It's lethargy! We walked into a place full of recycled hippy crap and this hippy British culture and said, 'Right, yeah, that's cool, like, I love my brother, but now let's do something bigger.' We did have an agenda — we had aspirations. But talk about a city with no ambition! Everyone might as well just have fucking rolled over and died."

The Hardkisses soon began looking beyond San Francisco in order to make a name for themselves. In 1991, Scott and Robbie released a record called *The Magical Sound of the San Francisco Underground* and made their intentions clear. They were going to *sell* this San Francisco vibe thing, the thing some thought the trio didn't actually possess. The Hardkisses installed themselves in a basement studio under a taqueria and set up Hardkiss Music. A hand-drawn tree of hearts became the label's logo. They put flaky slogans on the backs of their record sleeves and covered the fronts with full-color organicky graphics, from butterflies and batik patterns to flowers that look like Georgia O'Keeffe vaginas. At first, they recorded as a trio; then Scott recorded as "God Within," Robbie as "Little Wing," and Gavin as "Hawke."

Like the Chicago originators, the Hardkisses took exactly what they were hearing in the parties and clubs of the city they lived in and put it to vinyl: Jenö's aquatic breakbeats, disco from the gay clubs, and the shimmering, psychedelic, wah-wah grooviness of San Francisco's hippie history. Their productions, like God Within's classic "Raincry" (1993) or Hawke's more recent album *Namaquadisco* (1998), became early-morning favorites with both America's new-school dance society and scenes abroad, notably (ironically?) the one in the UK. This was a new kind of American house. It was not the direct product of a Black New York/Chicago/Detroit 1980s underground but a cousin once removed.

The musical tag "San Frandisco" was coined with the Hardkisses as figureheads. "Cute White boys making house music from San Fraaan Cisssco! The press loved us," says Scott Hardkiss, who, along with Gavin and Robbie, now holds a six-album deal with Capitol Records. "So, now, tell me. Which of these 'San Francisco rave pioneers' will people remember when we're all dead? When all these promoters and DJs die, who will remember them? All their talk will be — pouf! All gone. These people will be worm food. My records will be spinning round and round and round."

✦

Today, the Bay Area's major contribution to the American rave scene is coming from a group of people who've had nil to do with anything mentioned in this chapter: hip-hop scratch DJs, turntablists like the Invisibl Skratch Piklz (lead by four-time DMC DJ-competition champion Q-Bert), and recording artists like DJ Shadow, who have, in recent years, been instrumental in setting up a bridge of interest from rave into hip-hop culture. This, in turn, has helped create a new, and incredibly vibrant, strain of Vanilla B-boyism. The Hardkisses have remained the most globally successful and well-known figures to come out of the San Francisco rave boom. Wicked has only recently taken the inevitable, and somewhat belated, step into the studio, having set up two labels: Wicked and Greyhound Recordings. The rave scene still lives in San Francisco, albeit on a smaller scale. Martin O'Brien still promotes large-scale raves and is now called a "rave entrepreneur" by the new generation on the scene. The core group of the early nineties still throws the occasional party — usually small gatherings in little nightclubs or private lofts, the most popular of which are still the monthly benefits thrown for Malachy in his warehouse home.

3 TORONTO, CANADA
Hardcore Anglophilia and Jungle's
Northern Exposure

"Jungle, yeah, hardcore, the sound of our streets," says DJ Danny Henry. "We were pushin' it to the tits, we were, like, mad, tellin' people what the culture's really all about, yeah? There was a DJ, from Liverpool, named Malik X — he had a radio show called *Radio London*. Then there was Dr. No — he was a DJ and an MC, he did a lot of pirate radio in London an' that. We were educating people about our culture, *British culture*." Danny Henry is twenty-five years old. He used to be a DJ, but now he works at a Chrysler factory in Brampton, Ontario. Danny speaks with the broadest Glaswegian drawl you've ever heard. But Danny is not Scottish, and he's not talking about any scene in the British Isles. It's been close to a decade since Danny swapped his soft Canadian accent for a hard Scottish burr, since he got into raving through some Scottish friends and — like dozens of other Torontonians — decided it would be more appropriate to speak like a Brit and even sometimes pretend he was born across the pond.

The Toronto rave scene in the first half of the nineties encompassed one of North America's largest rave populations. To this day, the city remains one of the continent's more vibrant rave centers, serving as an outstanding example of how the imported culture of rave has been absorbed differently in different environments. In Toronto, rave was met with, as many Torontonians have told me, "No patriotism. We don't have patriotism." In American cities such as San Francisco or Los Angeles, where the first raves were realized mainly through the efforts of expat Britons, a process of Americanization usually took hold after a short period of British mimesis. In Toronto, the initial impulse to do what the British do never quite wore off. It still exists, and it has led to the creation of a rave scene quite different from almost any other in America.

Torontonians actually pride themselves on having a very British rave scene. Most of the important promoters in the city have been Britons. The initiators were a pack of teenage boys of Scottish origin who called their promotions company Exodus and, in 1991, introduced Toronto to the *über*-British sound of UK breakbeat-hardcore. Breakbeat-hardcore functioned as an early sound for many North American rave scenes; however, it was usually discarded and replaced by other house styles when hardcore began morphing into the unravey sound of jungle in the UK. But Toronto resolutely followed London's sonic lead. Fusing jungle, a Black, nonrave sound, into their completely White, very ravey, rave scene, Torontonians created what British magazine *i-D* crowned, in 1995, "the largest jungle scene in North America."

"People wanted to have a scene just like they have in England, so they just copied everything," says Toronto jungle DJ Ruffneck. "When other North American rave scenes cut the strings between [themselves] and the UK, Toronto never did. Toronto had come so far with hardcore, it was just natural to flow into jungle. The only difference is, no Black people here were interested in it, and they stayed away. So, in the end, the scene was pretty different from England's."

◆

Unlike its powerful American counterpart, the Canadian identity is a pretty wishy-washy number. A quick national-identity survey of young English-speaking Canadians yields similar sentiments over and over again: "We are not like Americans." Or, sometimes, mainly among Whites, "We are more like the British." The Anglo-Canadian habit of locating identity through comparisons to either Canada's superpower neighbor or Canada's mother country is widespread. Among the people I interviewed for this chapter — many of whom have no British ancestry whatsoever — one thing is certain, though: they generally like Britain more than they like the US. A couple of Toronto ravers I spoke to said that they even feel, much the way their grandparents do, that having the Queen of England as Canada's figurehead of state has been an important component in preventing Canada from being "absorbed" into the US.

In fact, UK-centrism is an old friend to Toronto youth culture. In the late 1970s, the UK punk of the Sex Pistols hit hard: "There were so many Union Jacks, yolk-styled Mohicans, and all that 'anarchyyyeeeea' stuff, the whole city seemed like a 'Greetings from London' postcard," says Gavin McInnes, editor of the Canadian youth-culture magazine *Vice*. A few years after that, the running joke in Canadian indie-music circles was that "Toronto didn't breathe through its nose" — a reference to the faux-Brit whine that poofy new-wave Toronto bands like the Payolas inevitably took on. "You wouldn't believe how many people I know here who . . . grew up religiously reading [British teenybopper magazine] *Smash Hits*," says Chemistry's Alex Clive, an Englishman who became a Toronto rave promoter. "There never seems to be any great leap of faith involved in absorbing anything British here."

Throughout the eighties, rock radio station CFNY, which specialized in "alternative music," was the favorite of Toronto teens. The big DJ at CFNY was a Londoner named Chris Sheppard, who played and promoted mainly British postpunk bands like the

Cure, the Smiths, and Siouxie and the Banshees, along with synth-poppers like Depeche Mode and, later in the eighties, baggy rave-rock Manchester acts like the Happy Mondays and the Stone Roses. Sheppard was something of a local hero — a bombastic man-about-town who wore a black Johnny Cash hat and oozed exotic charisma. "He made pop seem really exciting — all of these imported records he hyped up. He had a talent for, like, vibrancy," says Toronto techno DJ James St. Bass. "For all the kids in the suburbs who listened to CFNY — kids in Mississauga, Scarborough, Brampton — he was bringing them a whole fantasy world of cool music. New Order were huge here when most people in America probably had no clue who they were. Chris Sheppard's influence must have been immense."

The suburb of Brampton has a large Scots-émigré population. But, aside from the odd tartaned-up pub, it presents a fairly standard picture of middle-class North American suburbia: cookie-cutter housing developments inhabited by barbecue-apron-wearing adults and lots of children and teenagers; the population is heavily White. "Growing up in Brampton in the eighties was really, really boring," says DJ Ruffneck — Steve Ellul to his mom and dad. "It was all Burger Kings. Dairy Queens. I hung out at the 7-Eleven for about two years: pull up, case of beer, parking lot, drink on the curb. Typical Canadian suburbia. Then the Scottish thing started happening in 1991."

The "Scottish thing" was, in the beginning, a mix tape at a teenagers' party in someone's rec room. The cassette had been imported from Scotland by a newly landed eighteen-year-old named Anthony Donnelly. "I'll never forget it," says Ruffneck. "Anthony Donnelly threw in this tape. We were all convinced that it was the best music we'd ever heard. It was pure British hardcore, like, the hardest, fastest stuff ever. Anthony was beaming. He said, 'That's it, we're gonna throw a real party and play this.' We had no clue what 'this' was, but it sounded exciting." The Brampton crew, lead by Donnelly and his best friend, another expat Scot named John Angus, started going into Toronto on weekends to see what they could find.

"We were going around Toronto warehouse parties. At first, it was five or six of us, but every weekend it would escalate: it became ten, fifteen, twenty, thirty people, all from Brampton," says Angus. "We went out to warehouse parties and gay bars in Toronto looking for Ecstasy, and no one would sell [it to] us. They were just, like, [camp voice] 'I'll give *you* ecstasy,' swatting our asses and stuff. Eventually, we ended up finding Ecstasy — I mean the drug — and realized we had to set up our own thing. We couldn't find the music we liked, and we had, like, dozens of kids following our lead every weekend. We were a *heavy* crew!"

When the Bramptonians descended, Toronto's house scene, centered on gay clubs and illegal soulful warehouse parties dubbed "booze cans," was covered top to toe in deep New York house. "Toronto was one of the earliest cities for house in North America. It's a pretty short drive from here to New York," says Peter Primiani, owner of 83 West Records and one of the first house DJs in the city. "We played lots of Garage classics, the soul vocals, with a lot of the Smack records, Blaze records, Masters at Work, disco for the gays. It was classy."

"It was very exclusive and fashiony and bent on the whole cool-underground thing," remarks James St. Bass, a DJ who played the booze-can circuit before "going techno." "Then, in about 1991, we all started seeing these *British* guys show up at these soulful garage warehouses, in floppy fish hats, blowing whistles. Most of the warehouse people were not about this at all. 'Who are these children with the whistles?' Then we noticed they weren't just British, but *Scottish*. And they were multiplying. The multiplying Scottish disease. I think the little house clique was quite happy when these kids started Exodus. These Scottish Brampton people were like a style cramp for the housers."

The Brampton group found an after-hours club on the skids called 23 Hop, and they found some DJs. "There was a DJ playing who we'd met — Mark Oliver. The club he was playing at always gave him the last DJing slot of the night, because he played some hardcore, like bangin' techno, and it would clear the strays out and everyone could go home earlier," says John Angus. "He was Scottish, too, so we had a good laugh and decided to do something together. He could play; we would promote." The collective hired another British DJ — Black, dread-headed Londoner Neil Thomas, who went as Dr. No. He also played hardcore and was rumored to have been a pirate-radio jock in England. They called their weekly event Exodus and mainly featured the commercial, kiddie side of hardcore, which was also rising in popularity at that time among British suburban ravers. Saturdays at 23 Hop suddenly became wild stuff. "Rather than the usual fare of moody housers, poseurs and bummed-out B-boys, Exodus' crowd wasn't afraid to wig out," wrote an anonymous reporter in a 1992 issue of Toronto rave zine *The Punter*. "It was all kids from Brampton and Mississauga and Scarborough who just wanted to dance til dawn with their shirts off, dripping sweat, shouting at everyone and their dog!"

The Ecstasy, which the promoters took great care in distributing, helped. "We were pushing it," says Danny Henry, a behind-the-scenes aide at Exodus. "We were definitely pushing the Ecstasy thing — like, 'Go ahead. Try one. Get into it.' And that's how Exodus exploded." The scene was one of a high-school social gone berserk and slightly criminal. "Ach, it was so mental!" says John Angus. "All us Brampton kids — sixteen, seventeen, eighteen years old — runnin' round in our big trousers and kicker boots, Es straight from the best places, every kid with a whistle, staff on the bar, me an' Anthony runnin' out back at the end of the night with a sack o' loot! The beginnin'!"

Exodus was short-lived — it hung on for under six months — but it was point zero for the Anglomania that would endure within Toronto rave. The Brampton pack, following Angus and Donnelly, sought out UK-made clothing like Joe Bloggs jeans (the product of a UK sportswear company that specialized in the especially wide flares favored by Manchester ravers) and, a particularly cartoon-Limey touch, football jerseys and scarves. Brampton is a British place-name to start with, but, apparently, it wasn't British enough for the Exodus ravers: they began calling the inspirational suburb "Brampchester," making the connection to one of England's more obvious (yet not centralized) raved-up cities — Manchester. "The multiplying Scottish disease" James St. Bass refers to ("What were they? he asks. "Cousins? Cousins' cousins?") was not actually a case of multiplying Scots: it was a case of multiplying Scottish accents.

"That was the thing to do," says Ruffneck. "Soon, everyone was talking like a Scot at Exodus. I mean, people would be walking down the streets speaking perfectly good Canadian English, but the second they'd get to the party, the Scottish accents would be flying." Some even kept those accents permanently. "It was out of respect for Anthony and John and Mark Oliver, I guess. Like, pride that Exodus was really legit because of where [Donnelly, Angus, and Oliver] were born. Or maybe people wanting to get the same kinda reverence the promoters got because of their birthplace. It was a funny time."

◆

The "explosion" at Exodus was, in the grand scheme of things, really only the igniting of a pilot light. As the club's six-month heyday was coming to an end, the parents of the promoters were fighting outside the club, accusing each other's children of skimming money. The Exodus organization was not going to be taking Toronto to the next level. "They were kids," says Alex Clive, a North Londoner who was vacationing in Toronto in 1991. Clive decided to stay on, he says, "to basically make a rave scene, to synthesize a real rave crowd." Himself a kid when he landed, only twenty years of age, Clive was nonetheless an old hand at the party biz, having been an assistant since the age of sixteen to celebrated "style decade" club-promoter Philip Salon in London.

Clive was painfully aware of the cultural currency his nationality held in Toronto. Upon setting up his rave-promotions company, Chemistry, he immediately retitled himself "Alx of London" and set about specializing in one-off raves that promised many things. "UK." "Useful letters," says Clive, who is now a videographer for the Canadian arts television channel Bravo. Clive made Exodus's token London-born DJ, Dr. No, and a DJ originally from Liverpool named Malik X, his regulars. He flew in star DJs from England, like the Shamen's Mr. C, as well as the maker of the rave-anthem "Spice," Eon. He once paid twenty thousand dollars to have a Raindance rave being held in Essex broadcast live at one of his own raves via satellite and big screens. Clive introduced Toronto to full-color flyers, the kind used during the hardcore era in the UK. These were packed with inspirational messages ("Wake up and come alive!"), boasts about sound and wattage, and back-to-kiddieland attractions (bouncy castles, trampolines). And they were so riddled with check-out-my-British-lineage slang ("innit"?) and the "useful letters" U and K that they verged on parody. Clive even called one event the Back from the UK Rave after he's returned from a vacation back home.

"He was such a character," says DJ Patrick Dream, who was an aspiring teenage DJ on the booze-can circuit when he began helping Clive out. "He was the first real British person that I sat down with and talked with, and I was just fully impressed. I remember seeing him and Dr. No with their big, puffy Michelin Man jackets and their fuckin' Bluntstones [boots], and their style seemed so far ahead of everything else that was going on in the city. I was instantly taken in. So was everyone else."

An admitted "production obsessive," Clive was interested in creating total rave environments. He spent days spray-painting seascapes and attaching dangling fish cutouts to a warehouse ceiling for a Chemistry rave called 20,000 Leagues under the Sea.

He ordered hundreds of beach balls for one summer rave. He hired red double-decker buses as shuttles and covered up the windows so no one could identify the secret location of a rave called Magical Mystery Trip (maybe named in homage to Sunrise's famous Mystery Trip rave). At one point, Clive decided that he wanted to serve alcohol at an event, "for the older people to drink." He found a disused factory building, rented it three weeks in advance, and then beavered away with tools and plywood, building a second set of walls to line the immense room; the space between his plywood and the original walls was used to accommodate secret bars, which could be concealed behind sliding shutters. "You pulled one string and boom!" says Clive. "All the shutters would drop and the bars disappeared. Police-proof. It was amazing. I must have been out of my mind."

To an extent. One of the most extraordinary factors in Toronto's rave situation was the police. From the start, they assumed a nonreactionary stance, seeing the benefits of parties that could keep kids off the streets. After a short investigation of rave parties, Sergeant Guy Courvoisier, who was in charge of the investigation, stated, "It's going to be a long, hot summer. Unemployment is high. People need something to do. Raves don't need to be a problem. They can be a solution."

At the beginning of the investigation, in April of 1992, the police called Alex Clive at home: "It was the day after I had started giving out flyers for the fourth Chemistry rave, [called] Chemistry 4. It was a Saturday, the phone rings, and it's a policeman at the 33 Division, a downtown division. 'Is this Alex Clive? We'd like you to come in and talk to us about something.' So I'm, like, shitting in my pants! The next day I walk into this interview room at Station 33 and there are two policemen there, plainclothes. The first thing they do is they put a flyer for Chemistry 4 down on the table. I just sat down, put my arms up in the air, and was, like, 'Well, you've got me. What do you want to know?' They didn't need to know anything — they had a file on me about three-quarters of an inch thick, and I had only done three parties. They knew who my friends were, everyone who worked for me, all the DJs, the date I came into the country. It was like a scene in a movie. I was so into my raves then, the only thing I cared about was whether I would be allowed to throw my next one. I had just spent two and a half thousand dollars on flyers. They said, 'Don't worry, you'll be able to throw your party. The reason we brought you in here is so that you can go back and make sure that everybody knows that we know what's going on.' They said the Toronto police force's attitude was quite simple: that they wanted the events safe and that they would rather have two thousand young people in a safe, controlled environment on weekends than running loose on the streets causing mischief. Before I left, they patted my back and said, 'Have a good party.' I walked away from that police station smiling from ear to ear. I was, like, 'I can not fucking believe this! I *love* this city!'"

◆

By 1992, Chemistry ranked among the best-known rave-promotions outfits on the germinating North American rave circuit, which was still confined to big cities — or, at least, key cities, such as state or provincial capitals. Culling punters from the housey booze-can scene, from the Exodus posse, and from under-twenty-one teen clubs, Alex Clive amassed a big enough crowd to keep his party head counts at a steady fifteen hundred. But, as 1993 approached, he had begun to lose interest in Toronto rave altogether. He explains that he was finding the scene "empty," and he was not making much money due to the cost of his productions and the fact that a couple of his events had failed.

Given his all-consuming passion for production, Clive had never spent loads of energy trying to infuse Toronto's budding rave scene with any sort of ideology or party purpose, aside from making the altogether standard references to love and unity. "Raves are fast becoming the biggest movement in youth culture of all time," offered a Chemistry flyer for a party called Lost in Space. "Breaking down the barriers of racial and social ignorance and, above all, *having a wicked time*. We believe this is the *true meaning of rave*." In Toronto, "having a wicked time" really was about as far as it went.

Toronto is a keenly utilitarian, in-your-face city. It feels like a very new city, having boomed into a fast metropolis in the seventies and eighties, usurping the romantic French city of Montreal in its role as the cultural capital of Canada when Montreal began having political troubles due to civil unrest between its majority French and minority English populations. "Toronto is very *shiny*, into the brand new. It is a lovely place to live, but it is also quite [self-]conscious and can be a little plastic-y," says Clive. "It is a city of very little subtlety." If an American counterpart has to be found, Toronto — now the film-industry, television-industry, and music-industry capital of Canada — might be matched with Los Angeles. Both cities thrive on cultural industries, and both are charged with synthesizing national culture and broadcasting it via screen, disc, tube; yet, in both of these centers, "culture" of the authentic, unmediated, rising-up-from-the-streets kind can often (but by no means *always*) seem inauthentic. "Plastic."

There are thus certain similarities to be found in LA's and Toronto's rave development. After a year or so of playing around with this meaning or that message, both cities eventually settled on scenes based upon the twin aspects of hedonism and sheer grandiosity. Rave as entertainment. A playground for grown-ups — or almost-grown-ups. A place to release yourself and have big fun. In Los Angeles, this resulted in hundred-thousand-dollar parties for which entire movie sets were erected in warehouses, or ravers were ferried out to "Gilligan's Island," or whole amusement parks were imported to rave sites. In Toronto, in 1992, when rave was blossoming into an industry — already spawning new clothing shops, record outlets, and soon even a heavily technofied dance radio station called Energy 108 — this shift towards the mega-mega-monster rave was also underway, albeit with a more UK flavor (Trip to Trumpton instead of Gilligan's Island).

The promotions outfit most responsible for the bigging up of Toronto rave was called Nitrous, the brainchild of seven partners, most notably a commercial-radio DJ named Don Burns. Burns "totally, readily, and one hundred percent" admits that he was primarily interested in making Toronto rave "go commercial." "Why take a great thing like rave and confine it to an underground?" he says in a voice so radio-friendly you'd think he was delivering a weather report. "I thought the whole idea of rave was *mass* enjoyment."

Burns's career as a radio jockey began in the early seventies ("I played album-oriented progressive rock"). He spent most of the eighties as a personality jock on Toronto and Buffalo, New York, stations, playing Top 40 and sometimes adult contemporary: Lionel Ritchie, Kenny Rogers, and Barbra Streisand. He says that his personal interest in "new forms of music" grew and grew during this time; he'd started feeling he "could do [his] Top 40/adult contemporary radio schtick in [his] sleep." In 1992, Burns was hired by Toronto's heroically influential CFNY (he was already the voice of CFNY's station IDs) as a weekend dance-music DJ. After less than six months, he moved to the new Energy 108. Burns had rechristened himself with the "cool" moniker Dr. Trance. On a business trip to Los Angeles in 1992, Burns attended a rave that would have a great influence on the Nitrous raves — "just because this LA thing was so over the top!" he says.

"There were five raves happening in LA that night," Burns continues. The city was really happening then. I was with a friend of mine who is a commercial radio DJ in LA. He had never been to one of these and did not know what to expect. The trail to the party was really freaky — a big plan to bamboozle the cops. You had to phone up a number, and then they gave you an address in West Hollywood, which turned out to be a costume shop. I thought, 'Jeez, this is a bad place for a party.' There were a couple of burly security guards out front letting people in, a couple at a time. When I went in, I put my money down, and they gave me a wristband and an invitation to a video shoot with a phone number on it. They told you to call the number. Conveniently, there was a phone right outside the costume shop, and the phone number gave you instructions on where to go — about fifteen miles into downtown LA. Then you had to pull into a parking lot where there was a limousine, and if you had a wristband on, the guy in the limousine gave you a map to the party, which was a couple of miles away in some kind of theater. . . . The place was mad and full of cool things! There were all these kids who had laser pens, which were going everywhere, and some people were selling Mad Hatter hats, which I had never seen before. There were all kinds of booths and attractions and amusements, and there was a water bar going along the entire length of the room. This was an expensive production!"

Some of the earlier Nitrous parties "took direct inspiration from that LA scene," says Burns. "We tried to do the same thing — all that crazy, confusing chase business to get to the party." But why? There were no problems in Toronto with the police. "No, but it seemed a very ravey thing to do. Only we didn't want to confuse people too much, so we just sent people to a parking lot and there was a guy there on a lawn chair who told you where the rave was."

Nitrous was a bit hokey. Its great plans for LA-worthy raves often went cockeyed or just seemed off or unsophisticated to the more savy, well-traveled Toronto raver. Burns and company once hired an amusement park, complete with a full-sized Ferris wheel, for an outdoor rave; they also enlisted a landscape designer, who devised an elaborate plan involving "color-coded" areas with gel-spotlit trees. But the Nitrous crew had not anticipated rainfall in the days leading up to their rave: within hours, all the rides had sunk into the soft, muddy earth — the Ferris wheel was at a forty-five-degree angle by 1 A.M. — and their designed landscape had been overturned and trampled. Nitrous would also sometimes set up buffets at raves where all anyone was likely to chew on was their lower lip or a pacifier. They had a *pig roast* at one, fully sponsored by the Loblaw's supermarket chain.

But still the raves grew and grew, eventually drawing crowds of multiple thousands. Soon, even Nitrous was feeling that its parties had gotten too big to handle, and the company changed its promotions name to Atlantis in order to get off to a fresh start. Atlantis's forte was throwing raves in "insane" places, like the Ontario Science Museum or the CN Tower, a Toronto landmark where security was extreme and a no-smoking policy had to be observed. These raves (all legal) appealed mainly to teenagers — teenagers who may have first learned about techno music by listening to Burns on the radio. Or by listening to Burns's close friend and Atlantis resident DJ Chris Sheppard. Sheppard — former alternative hero of CFNY — had gone pop-techno and was now the star DJ of Energy 108, making millions selling TV-advertised compilations, called *Chris Sheppard's Techno Trip* or *Have a Nice Trip*, that featured the commercial end of Euro hardcore.

Both Burns and Sheppard could never quite shake off their car-aaayyy-zee radio-DJ acts. Burns would wear wacky printed waistcoats, and when he hit the decks, he'd immediately pick up the microphone, a tool he insisted upon, and in a voice familiar to every radio listener in Toronto, he's warn: "This is Dr. Trance. Prepare to enter with me into the rave zoooone." Sheppard, who called himself DJ Dogwhistle when he played at raves, would always be dancing with a freaky "I'm raving! I'm raving!" vigor when behind the turntables. He would punch the air, wear zany hats, wink, put his hands in the air. He made it all look so effortless, partly because, crouching at his feet, there would always be a man mixing the records for him. Mixing was something Dogwhistle had never learned to do. "He was more a star," says Burns. "But he was very talented at choosing. Like a selector! A selector who put on a great show. The kids loved it."

◆

For a time, Nitrous ran things in Toronto. At the dawn of 1993, Toronto rave had become a tremendously large scene, but it was still an easy, orderly ride — a fun circus with fun Saturday-night drugs and fun music. The sound of hardcore was still omnipresent, with rave kids taking pride in their city's taste, wearing T-shirts bearing popular UK slogans like, "Hardcore. You know the score." "It was becoming really clear around then," says Rob Lisi of the Toronto rave-promotions company Syrous, "that hardcore was the sound of our city. It had not been replaced by anything else like it [was] in most American cities. Kids here got most crazy to those UK breakbeats — the very fast hardcore breakbeats, like the stuff on [British hardcore labels] Moving Shadow, Suburban Base: those records were the bomb for the kids."

In the winter of 1993, the UK's kiddiecore rave era effectively ended. "On the hardcore rave scene, the winter period linking 1992 to 1993 was *dark*," writes Matthew Collin in *Altered State*, his history of Ecstasy culture. "Nights closing in, pills deteriorating in quality, and the music changing to fit the crepuscular mood." The typical picture of the hardcore UK raver in this era is one of an emaciated, sunken-cheeked, wild-eyed tweaker, gurning from too many "crap Es." The toll taken by the speed sold as Ecstasy or the worrisome cocktails of mixed chemicals that hardcore ravers were ingesting was being acutely felt. Overdose cases increased dramatically; excess had reached a frightening pinnacle. Criminality and scamming had also rooted themselves in the hardcore arena by this time. "People were murmuring about stabbings and muggings," continues Collin, "nightmares on the edges of rave." The music on many of the top UK hardcore labels chronicled raving's deviation into darkness. Hardcore had entered a phase typified by horror-movie samples, tougher, more ferocious breakbeats, and ominous airs. The sound was called "darkside," or just "dark," or "darkcore" — dark hardcore — a title that would have been an oxymoron a year before but that now fit the speed-lagged atmosphere of the times.

As 1993 progressed, Nitrous found itself being edged out by a new company called Pleasure Force. With Pleasure Force at the helm, Toronto's rave scene changed dramatically: as it had in the UK, rave went rough and dark, not only in terms of sound but also structure and vibe. It's hard to say whether Toronto rave had simply come to the same kind of crisis as its British counterpart — only in a more condensed time frame — or if the "two-year honeymoon" rule applies here. It's also possible that the city had achieved some kind of weird synchronicity with Britain. "It was a dramatic turn: one day happy-happy, the next day very edgy and frightening," says Beverly May, publisher of Toronto-based techno zine *Transcendance*. "At Pleasure Force raves, you knew there was weird shit going on. You would see these people doing coke lines off tables and little kiddies on crystal meth hobnobbing with people in their late twenties. It was rotten by anyone's count. It was a place where you could do anything, and there were people there doing pretty much that . . . I thought it was vile."

Pleasure Force was primarily the concept of a thirtysomething Englishman named Alan Stevenson and a Canadian who had jumped ship from Nitrous named Mike Stein. Stevenson was also the owner of X-Static, an enormously successful shop off Toronto's fashionable Queen Street. X-Static was like a rave lifestyle center, selling tickets for parties, clothing (orange boiler-suits, phat pants), rave accessories (glo-sticks, whistles, record bags), a bit of vinyl, and a massive selection of DJ mix tapes (often bootlegged). Stevenson was believed to have extensive underworld connections, but he could be extremely benevolent with "the kids." He'd often lend younger local DJs the money to duplicate their latest mix tapes for X-Static, and he was a benefactor to those who wanted to design ravey clothing or accessories.

"He had an empire, down to the drugs," alleges Toronto jungle DJ Sniper. "Alan was even bringing the rave drugs in. He was [smuggling] E inside the [imported] mix tapes being sent to X-Static. Whoever was sending the tapes would take out some of the tape reels, and fill the shells with E, and then seal the tapes up again, and send 'em to X-Static. . . . That's how Alan was getting pills into the country. Like, how insane is that?"

Stevenson's Pleasure Force called one of its first parties Darkside. The drugs at the party were appropriately horrid. "I remember these purple E's going around that party. Nasty!" says John E, who was both resident DJ and a partner in Pleasure Force. "People were tripping way too hard! It was really dark, like in England." Pleasure Force organizers would never leave any party unaccompanied, says John E. "There was lots of money and lots of sketchy business. When we [the promoters] went home, we'd go in pairs and have a security guard with us. One night, we broke that rule, and the cash went home with one partner alone. We agreed that we'd divide it all in the morning. This guy then called half an hour later and said he'd been robbed. Things were so fucked that we didn't know if he stole it and was lying or if his story was legit. And he was a Pleasure Force *partner*."

The Pleasure Force raves would regularly lure over five thousand people, a big jump from Alex Clive's crowds of fifteen hundred only a couple of years before. The Pleasure Force crowd was notoriously young. Cocaine and strong speed like metamphetamine had worked their way into their circle. Ravers would stack meth over their Ecstasy and would often use other drugs like Valium, to come down at the end of the night. "Pleasure Forces were mega-hardass — so huge, and so bad. Every corner you turned there would be some guy: 'E, speed, E, speed, coke. . . .' I was seventeen at the time and loving it, fucked on crystal meth and Es, living for the Pleasure Force parties," says Andrew C., now a political-science student at a university in a major Canadian city.

"I remember this one party. I was cruising around, high as a fucking kite," continues Andrew, "and I saw a filthy girl sitting balled up in a corner. She was crying — she was on crappy E and she had soiled herself [defecated]. She must have been about sixteen. Anyway, I took her in the bathroom. The bass was going beuurm-beuurm-beuurm, shaking all the stalls, and there were a buncha guys in there cursing coz they had put their lines down on the sink surface and it was wet and their blow had instantly turned to mush. Anyway, I cleaned the girl up and then propped her up by the sinks, and I went to pee. When I came out, she was, like, practically fucking some other dirty rave kid in the corner of the bathroom — in front of everyone, no one cared . . . it was all so sketch[y]."

The dark Pleasure Force aura soon caught up with the promoters. Stevenson was forced to leave Canada in 1995, and the parties and X-Static were shut down soon after that. While investigating Stevenson for drugs, the police were rumored to have found child-pornography magazines and video cassettes in his possession. "It's said that the police actually found videotapes of Alan with these little ravers," says Beverly May, who believes that Stevenson was a closet homosexual, tortured by his impulses. "Alan's brother Amon came in to take over X-Static and Pleasure Force. Amon had no clue what he was getting into."

In 1995, Amon Stevenson hung himself. Some Toronto ravers still wonder if the death really was a suicide, or if Amon had been murdered by some of his brother's former business associates in a "settling of accounts." "I had started distancing myself from Pleasure Force long before then," says John E. "When the shit hit the fan, I took a one-eighty and looked the other way. . . . Everybody did."

◆

By the end of the Pleasure Force era, Toronto's ties to the UK were as close as ever. Alan Stevenson had brought in some of the UK's leading hardcore DJs — people like Kenny Ken, Jumping Jack Frost, and Randall — for raves, and X-Static's wall of DJ mix tapes imported from England served as a constant, direct channel between Toronto's massive rave population and the most underground of London sounds. "Those tapes, of [English DJs] like Mickey Finn, Grooverider, and DJ Hype, were a very important education for the city," says Rob Lisi. "I remember one tape sold thousands. It was of DJ Fabio and MC GQ. It was rerecorded from kid to kid to kid. I'm not kidding when I say there must have been seven thousand kids with that tape in Toronto. If it could have charted, if it would've: GQ — just an MC, for crissakes — became a superstar here. He was Michael Jackson!"

Lisi, a Portuguese Canadian, was in charge of the "record corner" at X-Static, and he'd stock all of the newest UK releases, especially the darkcore that was coming out on London labels like Suburban Base, Moving Shadow, Reinforced, Lucky Spin, No U Turn, and Ram. It was obvious to Lisi by about 1993 that the music he was stocking could no longer appropriately be called "hardcore techno." "The sound was changing, becoming all about the breakbeats, the drums, and the bass . . . there was also a lot of reggae business going on in the new tracks — dub bass lines, ragga samples." He says it was then that he first heard the word *jungle* used as a name for this new kind of hardcore, a form he "was becoming obsessed with." Lisi set up the rave-promotions company Syrous in 1994 with his brother Vito (who MCed at raves with a faux-Cockney accent using the moniker MC

Brocksy) and friend Chris Smart. Their intention was to throw raves that played only this fresh kind of hardcore called jungle.

Like rave itself, jungle was one of those stunning cultural combustions that nobody could have foreseen. The British media had completely blacked out rave and hardcore for most of the nineties, instead pushing more "tasteful" and "intelligent" genres of dance music, like the snooty and overblown progressive house. This blackout meant that for hardcore, commercial radio play was hard to come by. In London, illegal pirate stations like Kool FM, run mainly by Black DJs and MCs, were filling the gap. These MCs, some of whom had defected from Black reggae/soul pirates, pattered and toasted over hardcore records, sometimes in a thick Jamaican or Jamaican-sounding patois, adding a whole new dimension to the tracks, like a reggae-techno sound clash.

The tracks themselves changed dramatically between 1992 and 1994. In the darkcore era, the music had pushed away from hands-in-the-air feel-goodness, and soon the roughest bits — the hardness of the breakbeats, the sonic boom of the sub-bass — started coming to the fore. On the records played in London clubs like Sunday Roast, a new sampling vernacular was being heard more and more often — reggae, ragga, dance hall. Like the mix that was going on at the pirate stations, the sound was morphing into Jamaicanisms. And the crowd and the new artistic blood that was drawn to jungle was increasingly Black, with whole cliques coming out of UK hip-hop and reggae scenes.

Jungle was vibed up as "the sound of Black Britain," "the UK's answer to American hip-hop," and it began chiseling out its own character. Hardcore had E; jungle had ganja. Hardcore had raves; jungle had Sunday clubs. Hardcore had whistles; jungle had lighter salutes and even the odd gunshot salute. Hardcore's reputation was "White"; jungle's was "Black" — even though, as Matthew Collins points out in *Altered State*, the producers of both genres had always been of diverse backgrounds.

In 1994, it seemed probable that Toronto's jungle scene

would become a lot like London's. Here was a city that displayed Anglophilic tendencies and had one of the largest West Indian populations in the whole of North America. There were no pirates in Toronto, but there were (and are) college radio stations, many with wonderfully unruly playlists and few strict policies. As early as 1992, Dr. No — who often went home to the UK to buy records and seek inspiration — was MCing ragga-style over hardcore breakbeats on his Radio London show (with DJ Malik X) on college station CIUT. By early 1993, another Black CIUT DJ named Marcus had seen, in his own words, hardcore's "Black potential" and had begun to try luring hip-hop and reggae fans into Toronto's raveland.

Marcus launched a promotions company named Delirium. His aesthetic was raggatastic: Delirium's flyers were adorned with lions and ladies clad in red, green, and gold bikinis. Marcus's adverts never had the word *thing* spelled with a honky *h* before the *i*. Delirium offered the grinding, sexy Delirium dancers, reggae MCs all night long, R&B and hip-hop back-rooms, and Toronto's most jungalistic DJs, some with roots in Toronto's large West Indian sound-system culture: Himself, Dr. No, Medicine Muffin, Jungle PHD, Ruffneck, the Hrdcru, Don Renks. Yet Delirium's patrons remained overwhelmingly White. "The Black people were happy with their own scenes, with hip-hop and R&B," says Marcus. "It just didn't work. I think they saw jungle as a British-White thing because in Toronto it was attached to rave, which was totally White. Jungle just didn't speak to blacks here."

"The Black music scene's attitude to jungle was almost . . . obnoxious," remembers DJ Jungle PHD. "Earlier on, there was only one record store in the city, besides the few records at X-Static, that stocked the music: Play de Record on Yonge Street. But Play de Record was, like, a hip-hop/house place, and they didn't respect jungle; they just thought it was for 'stupid rave kids,' so they would only carry a few releases every week. On

Thursdays, the owner would come out with one milk crate of jungle records. He would stand there laughing as all us DJs would lunge at it like crazed dogs, grabbing anything we could get our hands on. It was pathetic."

Syrous's first party, in May of 1994, was called Judgment Day. The party did not link together a new crowd, but it attracted the same ravers as any other techno DJ event would have. Still, "Judgment Day opened up everyone's eyes to this new music. And from then on, it was just like a chain reaction," says Lisi, who still throws supersized jungle events regularly. "By the time we threw our next party, the kids had dropped all their ravey stuff and started doing jungle things, like flicking lighters, and calling for rewinds on records, and winding and grinding. They may have been White, but they knew what to do."

Syrous teamed up with London's (shop and label) Lucky Spin Records for this next party, which featured a vast (and expensive) roster of UK jungle luminaries: DJ Rap, Darren Jay, DJ Hype, DJ Trace, Jumping Jack Frost, Slipmaster Jay, and LTJ Bukem. Five thousand people attended. In the short span between Judgment Day and this party, a new local DJing elite had surfaced in Toronto, as well, led by brothers Chris and Patrick Brodeur, who DJed as Sniper and Mystical Influence. "There was a short period where lots of the local jungle DJs were Black — Delirium and all that," says jungle DJ Spinz. "But with Syrous, the DJs coming up, like Sniper and Mystical, were White — former ravers. And those are the people who have kept the jungle scene alive here: White people. I don't want to sound pompous, but it kinda proves that there's no such thing as universally Black or White music. There's no DNA programming telling people what to like or what scene to be a part of."

But, as was suggested by one British journalist sent to Toronto to research an article on Canadian jungle, there may have been door policies and unspoken rules that indicated what scene a person should be a part of. "Everybody knows that in many

The Androgyny and the Ecstasy: Pete Avila and Doorman at Osmosis (San Francisco, 1990)
COURTESY PETER AVILA

Doc Martin – up for peace and equality – in New York City (c. 1989)
COURTESY DOC MARTIN

Acid Evangelist: Alan McQueen at a Tonka event in England,
just prior to departing for San Francisco
COURTESY GARTH WYNNE-JONES

Hooray for Mother Earth!! San Fran ravers getting groovy outdoors (c. 1991)
COURTESY GARTH WYNNE-JONES

"In California, nobody needs sweaters!" DJ Markie Mark at a Tonka event (England, c. 1989)

Hang gliders not shown: DJ Garth plays a Full Moon Rave (Bonnie Dune, 1993)

Techno-Spiritualism for sale: a booth at a Toon Town Rave (San Francisco, 1992)
GABRIEL ACCASCINA / LIAISON AGENCY

Look, Mum, no hands! Chris Sheppard in the "mix" (Toronto, 1996)

Toronto DJ Don Burns as his "wacky" alter-ego, Dr. Trance
ALEX DORDEVIC / TRIBE MAGAZINE

Aural Fixations: Toronto ravers suck!
ALEX DORDEVIC / *TRIBE MAGAZINE*

Dub Plate Pressure: DJ Sniper (Toronto, 1998)
ALEX DORDEVIC / *TRIBE MAGAZINE*

Lay back and think of England: Toronto Ravers at rest
ALEX DORDEVIC / *TRIBE MAGAZINE*

Original Nutter: Toronto Jungalist Dr. No (c. 1992)
GIVEN TO THE AUTHOR

Before: Drop Bass Network flyer (1992)
COURTESY KURT ECKES

After: DBN "Shake hands with the big guy downstairs"
COURTESY KURT ECKES

Nosebleed: Milwaukee raver takes Elmo into hardcore territory
COURTESY *MASSIVE*

Tommy Sunshine alive in Atlanta
COURTESY *MASSIVE*

The friendly citizens of America's dairyland: Wisconsin ravers at Even Further (1998)
COURTESY *MASSIVE*

The Devil made me do it: Kurt Eckes and Wife, April (1998)
COURTESY *MASSIVE*

A bloodied Matt Massive protests the presence of the Teletubbies,
at the Drop Bass Network New Year's Party (1998)
COURTESY *MASSIVE*

Remains of the day: Massive's "Sound System" after enduring Even Further (1998)
COURTESY *MASSIVE*

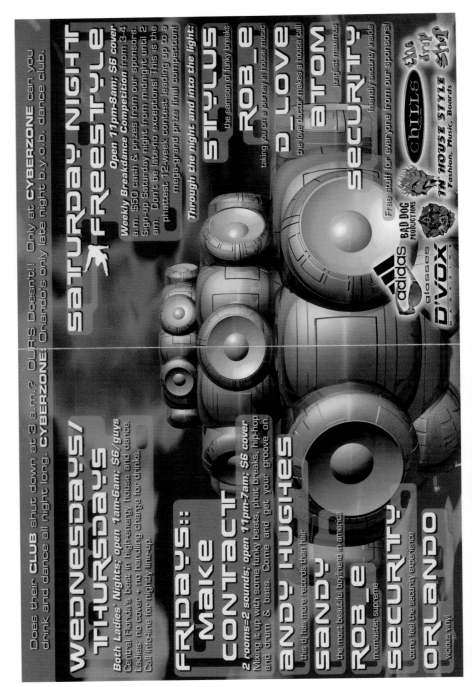

Open all hours! Cyberzone promotes Breaks and their Latenite license (Orlando, 1997)
COURTESY DAVID McWHERTOR

House of Blues: the "Historic" Firestone (Orlando)
PETER COSGROVE / CP PICTURE ARCHIVE

Rohypnol survivor: ex-Firestone bartender Eli Tobias (Orlando, 1998)
GIVEN TO THE AUTHOR

Birds of a feather . . . revellers at the Palm Springs White Party
VICTOR R. CAIVANO / CP PICTURE ARCHIVE

Sea of love: the Leather Ball, part of Montreal's Black and Blue Festival (1998)
LUC RICHARD / BAD BOY CLUB

trendy nightclubs in North America there are ceilings on how many Black people can get in in a night," says Toronto jungle MC Trigger. "I guess there's no reason to believe that that kinda thing couldn't go on at Toronto raves as well, even jungle raves. Often the security companies are the same at raves as in the nightclubs. But, even saying that, I wouldn't go around shouting 'racists!' at the jungle scene. That's way too simplistic. The new DJs like Sniper and Mystical Influence weren't coming up coz they were White; they were coming up coz they were the [Syrous] promoters' friends. The promoters and the kids would've been cool with an [interracial] thing — they probably even wanted it. Half those jungle kids were going around mackin' like they were niggaz anyway. It's just there was more interest in the scene from the Whitey kids. Trust me, there weren't all these tons of Black people going 'fuck hip-hop' and trying to bang down jungle's doors. I really think the doors were open to everyone."

◆

Jungle was not a big crowd pull in most rave scenes in the US and Canada. In most cities, the sound was only taken up by small cliques at jungle nights in little clubs or in the backrooms of some raves. Jungle's more-intellectualized, less-ghettocentric, less-raggatastic offspring — drum & bass — has done slightly better, but on a thoroughly collegy, nondance, alt-music-appreciation, at-home, CD-collector level.

Yet in Toronto, where the favorite sound remains the jump-up sound of 1993–94 ragga-jungle (the scene's all-time most popular record remains 1994's "Dead Dread," by Dred Base), a mutant, runaway culture has ensued. The jungle-rave scene in Toronto is still among the most vibrant and populated rave scenes in North America today. Syrous and (Syrous spin-off) Renegades parties now attract close to ten thousand patrons a pop, and new jungle DJs and producers, like the teenage tag team of Slip 'n Slide, are emerging continuously. Hilfigerized White kids and, increasingly, Black and Asian kids, are break dancing to MCS who now fake both Cockney and Jamaican accents at raves. Sniper and Mystical Influence have set up a record label called Vinyl Syndicate, and their productions have found favor with the hard-to-impress production enclave in the UK. The brothers have also established a record-distribution company called Fully Loaded, which is one of the main suppliers of jungle and drum & bass imports to record shops across North America.

"I'd like to believe," says Sniper, "that when jungle and drum & bass have run their course in England, which may have already happened, Canada could be the place that keeps jungle alive. That would be so cool. Then we could say our country gave more to music than just Bryan Adams and Celine Dion. Yeah . . . that would be really, really cool. Put us on the map, you know?"

4 THE MIDWEST
White Chicago, Black Milwaukee, and the Case of the Raving Satanists

The greatest boost to Milwaukee's rave culture has been the fact that there is nothing much to *do* in Milwaukee. Not many venues. Limited nightclubs. Few local bands. Not many DJs. And hangouts are scarce — unless you include antler-bedecked *biergartens* where crackling TVs blare from opening 'til closing. The city is both depressed and depressing. The police are notoriously racist. Racial segregation is entrenched. Unemployment is sky-high, primarily because the breweries that sprang from the city's great stream of German settlers in the nineteenth century moved off in search of cheap Mexican labor in more recent years. The only major brewery left in this Wisconsin town that beer made famous is Miller; located close to the center of Milwaukee, it spreads a sickly, tangy, yeasty odor over half of the city every single afternoon and evening. Charm is hard to find in Milwaukee. Futurism is even harder to trace — most shop signs look as though they date from decades back; their hand-painted lettering is peeling off, the victim of years of yeasty soot. Greasy-gray Formica diners cluster on street corners. Bus stations and banks look dilapidated. Even the airport looks haggard, empty, and dull, perched at the end of a cracked-up highway, a raised road lined with high concrete smokestacks, that nobody ever uses anymore. Shining America, this is not.

Milwaukee is a postindustrial problem. A dead city, a real one. And it's creepy. Doomsday prophets in big, black station wagons bearing slogans like, "Our day has expired!" prowl the streets. The cabdriver who took me into town informed me that "[conspiracy magnate] Art Bell is the sanest man in America," and asked if I knew that Wisconsin had the highest concentration of serial killers per capita in the country. He went on to tell me that the hotel I was staying in was the one where serial body-chopper Jeffrey Dahmer used to "meet his victims." The hotel staff confirmed the Dahmer bit. When I told Kurt Eckes — the main person I am in the Midwest to interview — this tidbit, he replied, "Spooked, huh? Yeah! Good! Welcome to Milwaukee!"

Eckes, the brains behind the remarkable rave-promotions outfit Drop Bass Network, is the most successful and celebrated promoter to come out of the Midwest rave scene, which exists within a circuit of cities that includes Milwaukee, Madison, Minneapolis, and Chicago. Originally from a rural-Wisconsin town, Eckes developed a rave vision that, hand in glove, fit Milwaukee's taste for dark music: metal from thrash to death, plus dirgy "heaviosity" rock. Eckes's body is covered in Marilyn Manson and Black Flag tattoos. He loves Kiss, Crü, Sabbath: he *is* metal. And the music he introduced first to Milwaukee and then to the rest of the Midwest has been termed "heavy-metal techno" by some — ferocious Belgian hardcore techno, Dutch and German gabba, Brooklyn hardcore, and an accompanying cast of terrorcores, deathcores, and speedcores, hard acids and hardcore acids. Dark, shattering mayhem music to go mental to. Noise that sounds as sinister as pounding jackhammers, swarming bees, and exploding bombs; techno so harsh and stomper-romper it's often described as "nosebleed."

Eckes also introduced the Midwest to his somewhat funky version of Satanism, informed equally by Anton LaVey's Church of Satan and good ol' rock mythology. In Milwaukee, ravers talk about dancing under giant goat heads and pentagrams at Drop

Bass Network parties as if these decorations were nothing more than pin spots. For years, they've shopped at record stores that also distribute cool flyers promoting hell and Satan. They've head-banged to techno. They've found fave rave drug Ecstasy "too soft," preferring the heavy pulse of LSD. They've gone through phases where everyone who's anyone dances with their heads inside the bass bins. Traveling through the urban decay of Milwaukee, it's easy to forget that farmland exists about twenty minutes out — Wisconsin is, after all "America's Dairyland" — and so, amazingly, many of these scenes of techno carnage have happened in barns, often surrounded by voluminous amounts of cow dung.

"I guess the Satan stuff may have seemed tongue-in-cheek to everyone outside Milwaukee, but it was real to us," says Eckes. "This is what we were all into. We started doing the Devil stuff and then [Midwest rave zine] *Massive* started doing it, and it became a daily part of our regular life, the bond of the time. Everyone walked around with the Devil. It was what set us apart from the rest. It was our identity. We were happy with that."

✦

One of the more surprising things about the 1990s Midwest rave circuit is that Chicago is a part of it and yet the history of 1980s gay-Black Chicago house did not directly inform it. The major points of inspiration for Kurt Eckes and the Midwest Hardcorps group of DJs and producers rallying around his Drop Bass Network are to be found not only in the Storm Raves of New York, but also in European rave — notably the rave scenes of Germany and the Lowlands, the sounds coming out of places like Belgium.

While it might seem weird that Belgium was a center for any kind of influential dance music at all, even weirder is the fact that one great, seminal strand of the Belgian techno sound originated in New York. Joey Beltram was one of the favorite

Storm Rave DJs. Some of his early techno tracks could not find a home imprint in America, and so they ended up being released on the Belgian label R&S. The most notable of these was *Mentasm* (1990), a record featuring a cold, swarming-buzz sound, which proved inordinately influential in Belgium. It led to the creation of the spooky "Belgian Hoover" sound (try to imagine a vacuum sucking up the sound of a choral record), heard on such Belgian hardcore records as Human Resource's "Dominator" (1991) and Traumatic Stress's "James Brown Is Dead" (1991).

With the Beltram tracks as catalyst, the Euro techno sound loudly 'n proudly moved away from Black America's housey spiritual booty shake. And, unlike the scene in England, this scene was also traveling away from the happy/kooky, flying in a rather more sinister, dark, industrial direction. The Hoover sound eventually turned into an all-round appreciation for harsh distortion and noise; the extreme pinnacle of this is to be found in gabba, the German hardcore techno that is distinguished by a pounding, distorted kick drum; a mean, terroriffic vibe (track titles: "Fucking Hostile," "Extreme Terror," "Cunt Face"); and BPM that can range from a fast-as-fuck 170 to an astonishingly fuck-off 300.

Gabba exploded in the northern bits of Europe and in France. It never really caught on in England (which, remember, had its own version of hardcore — breakbeat hardcore), but pockets of appreciation did crop up in the US: in Brooklyn, through the Storm Rave crew, which would heavy-metalize the gabba sound and retitle it "Brooklyn hardcore"; and in the Midwest, where gabba met the Wax Trax! industrial tradition of Chicago, toughened 303 acid squelches, and became hard acid, the area's favorite sound, primarily through the efforts of the Drop Bass Network and affiliated DJ/producers like Minneapolis's Woody McBride and Chicago's Delta 9.

✦

Euro-influence aside, this Midwest story is pretty much an all-American tale. The Midwest taste for heavy metal in dance started long before gabba was invented, even before the first Storm Rave occurred. A seminal spot for the hard-dance synthesis was a Chicago club — not the Warehouse, not Ron Hardy's "harder" Music Box, but an alternative establishment called Medusa's, where house music was played alongside industrial, punk, and metal, and the crowd was mainly White.

Kurt Eckes, who was so passionate about Medusa's that he bought up relics from the club when it closed, learned about house music there. So did many of the kids who would become his patrons. "Being White, straight, and from the Chicago suburbs, being the type of kid who wore Guns n' Roses T-shirts, there was no way I could have ever found out where the Warehouse was," says former Midwest raver Tommie Sunshine. "I mean, the way I found out about house — I think the way most White kids in Chicago found out about it — was by reading about what was going on in our city in the British [music weeklies] *Melody Maker* and *NME*."

Tommie Sunshine was born in Naperville, thirty-five minutes out of Chicago. He insists he was your "typical suburban Midwest youth" until, in his twenties, he earned the dubious privilege of being able to say that he went to almost every important rave thrown in the Midwest between the years 1991 and 1994 ("I was a rave celebrity"). "The join between the me who camped out all night for Kiss tickets and the me who became a tweaked-out raver was Medusa's," he explains. In 1987, a friend introduced him to the weekend house mixes on radio stations such as WBMX and WGCI, where the Hot Mix Five played. "After that, I'd be sleeping outside for heavy-metal show tickets with my Walkman on. And it's funny, because dance music, in my world, only existed on Friday and Saturday nights in my Walkman.

There was no place for kids like me to go dance. Let's be serious — there was almost no way to crack Chicago's Black house underground when you were so far out of the loop."

"It was very segregated," continues Sunshine. "I remember, once, coming out of somewhere late at night and getting a little paper flyer. It said, 'DJs Derrick Carter, Spenser Kinsey, Mark Farina' and had an address on the north side of Chicago. My friend and I knew the word *rave* by then; we figured this would be like the parties with the big smiley faces in England. So we went. We walked up a big flight of stairs and stepped into a room that was almost completely filled with Black [people], predominantly gay, with one strobe light and a lot of heavy, heavy house music. People were, like, 'Who the fuck are these kids?' At first we thought we were crashing somebody's house party. In a way, we *were* crashing someone's house party, actually. And we tried, but we had a very hard time tracking that scene again."

Soon, Tommie Sunshine and loads of White youths like him, who listened to house on Chicago radio, who were interested in the house music NME and *Melody Maker* had told them came from their own hometown, found Medusa's. "The club was the most amazing of meeting points," says Kurt Eckes: a three-floor roll-up containing a rock stage where bands like the Circle Jerks, Suicidal Tendencies, and Fugazi would play, a video room where music vids would run on all four walls (not Madonna — more like Stigmata), and a dance arena. Terri Bristol and Neil Strauss, who is now well known for being Marilyn Manson's biographer, were the main DJs.

"It was such a crazy musical mix," says Tommie Sunshine. "The Medusa's DJs would play not only Mister Fingers and Phuture and Marshall Jefferson and Adonis and all the early Chicago house, but also Ministry, Nitzer Ebb, all the Razormaid records, Nine Inch Nails, heavy industrial rock, heavy doomy Euro electronic stuff, some metal, *and* house stuff, in no particular order. Nobody thought it strange at all. You know, new wave was done, industrial was losing ground, and raving wasn't anything yet, either. We were like this weird midsection. I mean, I distinctly remember wearing Girbaud jeans that came up past my navel, a black-and-white polka-dotted shirt with a silk vest and my hair slicked back. Either that or a triple-extra-large De La Soul T-shirt. That was me. Surrounded by lots of Mohawks. It was the late eighties. I guess in Europe they had things all figured out by then, but us White folk in Chicago? We were still confused."

◆

Medusa's influence on Midwest rave did not immediately make itself felt. The situation in the Midwest was like it was in many other American centers. Rather than being primarily influenced by local clubbing experience, the first raves followed the toy-towny British 1990–92 how-to-rave model — the most obvious choice — and the result was what people in the Midwest now derogatively term "candy raves." The first of these capital-R Midwest raves went down in Chicago in October of 1991, at mythical rock venue Cabaret Metro. The driving force was Wade Hampton, a somewhat-nomadic dance-culture entrepreneur who had done E while it was still legal in Dallas, thrown some of the earliest techno one-offs in LA, and helped launch the Hardkisses in San Fran. This party Hampton concocted was called Fresh Jive, and it was sponsored by the Fresh Jive apparel company.

"Wade brought the Fresh Jive guys to Chicago for the party. Superstars!" says Tommie Sunshine. "Like, DJ Keoki and John Digweed and Scott Hardkiss were on the bill, and no one cared. But those Jive guys! They came with all their clothes and set up a stand where they were selling their T-shirts and hats. We couldn't believe it was real. It was the first time we had ever seen clothing that was made in America, for our lifestyle. We were begging all our friends to borrow money so that we could buy more stuff."

To the nineties American raver, Fresh Jive became what Lacoste was to the eighties preppy, what Hang Ten was to the seventies surfer, or what Fred Perry was to the sixties mod. It was a kind of cotton badge of certification, as powerful a unifying force as any important DJ or record or promoter. "You saw someone on the bus. You saw a Jive logo stitched on their clothes. You knew they'd be the same place you were that weekend," says Sunshine. Launched in California in 1990 by a young graphic designer named Rick Klotz, the company produced T-shirts Klotz says were inspired by 7–11 itself and the convenience-store chain's stock of Wacky Pack cards, Big Gulps, and sugar-zap cereals. By around 1992, Klotz's designs had induced a nutsoid trainspotter-ism in North America ravers. Kids would wait for the next batch of Fresh Jives to hit the one or two shops that carried the stuff in their town, then snap them up within days: brown-striped phat pants, toques and caps bearing pop-arty patches, and, most popular of all, T-shirts with detergent/cereal-box logos — the so-commercial-it's-underground supermarket imagery that also became a popular and enduring element of rave-flyer design in America.

"The night of Fresh Jive, we were there with a bag of lollipops, ready to fuckin' *rave*, man!" says Sunshine. "Ecstasy had not arrived in my world yet. That night, I robo'd — I drank a bottle of Robitussin — because I couldn't find real drugs." The party was a sensory production. Wade Hampton had decorated the Cabaret Metro floor to ceiling with tenting, onto which he projected movies and cartoons. On the stage where bands usually played, he'd piled close to forty television sets, all showing lunar landings and deep-space footage. "I remember saying to my friends, 'I'm *home*. Look around: this is all *ours*,'" says Sunshine, who believes that the group most attracted to rave in the Midwest was the "freaky kids who ate their lunches alone in the cafeteria. People who probably felt like outsiders."

In Chicago, where you can supposedly pay off the police with a pack of smokes, the Fresh Jive-style candy raves took off. They happened in elementary-school basements, skating rinks, and loft complexes. Corporate-logo mania continued throughout 1992; there were parties called Gatorave (featuring a flyer that looked like a Gatorade label) and Raveyear (snatching the Goodyear logo). "Personalities" like Tommie Sunshine, who soon took to wearing size fifty-two overalls and keeping a fuzzy Muppet in his back pocket, were emerging, too. A guy named Bob Smiley used to arrive at Chicago parties with a nitrous tank and sell balloons full of the laughing gas for five bucks. Smiley would also tour the dance floor carrying a four-foot inflatable toothpaste tube and bonk people on the head with it, egging them on as things started peaking.

Candy raves spread to Minneapolis and Wisconsin's homey state capital, Madison, in the spring of 1992. In Madison, they often happened in decorated barns. Parties were called Ravee (featuring the Borden Cow as mascot, a Dairyland ha-ha) and Alice in Raveeland (Borden Cow meets nineteenth-century LSD lit). At sunrise, as fingers of light penetrated the cracks in the barn walls, ravers would wander out to the pasture to pet the cows and horses.

In the summer of 1992, Kurt Eckes decided to move into a warehouse so that he could throw raves cheaply in his own pied-à-terre. He wanted to launch a scene in Milwaukee. For their first party's flyer, he and his housemate, Patrick Spencer, copied the M&M wrapper, only they turned the Ms on their sides so that they read "E&E": "a delicious pure bass center smothered in rich headstrong energy dipped in wonderful, blissed out ecstasy." Eckes and Spencer DJed at the party; Eckes called himself "Jethro X" and Spencer chose "Jedidiah the Messiah." They thought these were "funny hick names, Bible-belt names," says Eckes. "You know, it was *ironic.*" Now thirty-two, Eckes rolls his eyes when he shows me the E&E flyer. "Totally uncool," he says. "Uncool," and hardly a foreshadowing of what his and Spencer's rave company, the Drop Bass Network, would be doing a year later.

◆

It is in this era of the candy rave that the rave cities of the Midwest began linking up to form a circuit. The word *Midwest* might, for some, conjure up the idea of "small" — small-time, small-town, small-minded — but the geographic reality of the place is anything but. The American Midwest is several times the size of the entire United Kingdom. It takes six hours to drive from Milwaukee to Minneapolis, seven hours from Minneapolis to Madison or Chicago. Nonetheless, by 1992, Midwestern promoters had noticed that ravers were willing to travel megamiles through long stretches of bland cow-horse-cow-horse-barn-barn-barn scenery in hot pursuit of the next party, and they had begun advertising their events accordingly.

"The very act of driving became a huge part of the culture here," says Matt Bonde, editor of Milwaukee techno zine *Massive*. "Nobody traveled the way we did in the Midwest. Pretty soon, we were traveling even outside the Midwest, majorly cross-country. I remember leaving for Kentucky one Friday — that's a twelve-hour drive, by the way — just because we were bored. People in, like, New York [City], would never do that. They won't even drive to Jersey for a party. But when there is very little to do in a place, like in Wisconsin, you can become obsessive; whatever you are doing means more to you. So, to us, a car was freedom, and driving a total of twenty-four hours was a small price to pay for eight hours of raving."

In the fall of 1992, promoter Kurt Eckes and professional raver Tommie Sunshine met at a rave. They became fast companions after discovering that they had both started their clubbing careers at Medusa's. "Kurt seemed like a metal-rock hick with a thick Wisconsin accent to me," says Sunshine. "He didn't seem to come from happyland, but I liked him anyway." They soon started traveling together. Eckes would drive from Milwaukee to pick up Sunshine in Naperville on Friday, and they would return Monday morning. They were usually lucky enough to find places to crash, and they did most of their washing and primping in Denny's bathrooms or eerie highway rest stops. In December of 1992, they decided to make an extra-long trip to attend something really special. Both had read about New York's Storm Raves in Heather Heart's *Under One Sky* magazine. A pilgrimage was in order.

The journey, by rented van, took over a dozen hours. The Storm Rave — the last one ever — was held in a Staten Island stable. The experience (which is described in full in the prologue to this book) was nightmarish or wondrous, depending on which member of the Midwest contingent you speak to. Sunshine was nervous about the apparent street gangs that seemed "hard and dark and mean" and the "kids smoking crack." The music was new to him, harder and "scarier" than anything he had ever imagined; he was "in disbelief" over the walls of sound Storm Rave had installed for the party, too — speaker stacks so overpowering that they could burst eardrums. "I had never really heard hard-as-fuck, European-style, gabba-hardcore before," he confesses. Storm Rave had gone Euro-pummeling-hardcore by this point, and so Sunshine found himself subject to the meanest, most extreme DJ lineup that anyone outside Belgium or Germany could have conceived at that point: the core Storm DJs Jimmy Crash, Adam X, Frankie Bones, and Lenny Dee. When Jimmy Crash played, says Sunshine, "every record had a woman screaming, or ambulance sirens, or cursing in German, or babies crying. . . . Scary, mean drug music — it was evil."

Eckes's reaction was different. "That Storm Rave was a revelation," he remarks. "I was, like, 'This is exactly what I like!' It was the music that I liked, the atmosphere, the whole vibe. I just couldn't believe that they had a whole night of music focused on one sound. I was, like, 'We can do this thing. This is what I want to do. This kind of music. This kind of *everything*.'" Sunshine says, "Kurt was running around like a five year old at Christmas. In pure ecstasy. He had never seen anything that appealed more to him in his whole life. This Storm Rave was the exact point where he and I went north and south. That night, in that dark place, Kurt discovered his vision. . . . He shook hands with the big guy downstairs, and I decided that wasn't such a hot idea."

"A few months after that Storm Rave," says Eckes, "I resolved to stop fucking around. We [Drop Bass Network] did our one-year anniversary party, and it was all hardcore, like German hardcore, just like Storm Rave. We had to do it right, so it was in a horse barn, and the barn had a dirt floor, and [we] got a huge, huge sound system that took up one whole end of the place, like Storm Rave had. I was trying [to] totally emulat[e] what I saw there, coz I just couldn't fake liking all that everyone-together-happy-Midwest-vibe stuff anymore — so many people, just clueless, walking around thinking some grand interpersonal connection really exists in raves. Coming from my background — you know, metal, punk — it was incredibly annoying to me. I figured there is always a yin and yang, and if there's nobody promoting negativity and darkness in raves, then we [Drop Bass Network] have got it all to ourselves. I knew the combination could, should, exist. Not this light Ecstasy hedonism stuff, but real hedonism — like, decadence, in the classical sense."

◆

By the winter of 1992, the Midwest rave scene was already in a pretty somber situation due to a Halloween party that had gone down in Milwaukee called Grave Rave. The Milwaukee police had been easy on the scene until this event, but then they staged something of an intricately planned ambush. "The police came in, the lights came on, the police brought in desks and chairs, coffeemakers and snacks for themselves, plus several garbage bags of plastic cuffs, the kind usually used to keep cow legs together at slaughter time," says flyer designer Cody Hudson, a Grave Rave patron. "Boys and girls were separated into two areas and made to sit on the floor. We were not allowed to talk and would be barked at if we did, even if we smiled." The Grave Ravers sat in that unheated warehouse for over six hours, until everyone was charged. Some of the males dressed in Halloween drag were made to sit with the girls. "Standard Milwaukee police racism," says Hudson. They were fined $350 each for aiding and abetting in the illegal sale of alcohol, "even though no booze was sold at the event, and the police only found a total of nine bottles of beer behind the DJ booth, probably [the property] of the lighting crew." The ravers were then carted off to jail for the night, simply for being at a kegless keg party. All one thousand of them. On drugs, and in fancy dress.

The December 1992 cover story of Chicago rave zine *Reactor* was dedicated to the "MPD Rave." It bore the melodramatic headline, "They might stop the party but they can't stop the future." Yet most promoters in Milwaukee and the surrounding area were dropping out fast, fearful of a Grave reprise. The Drop Bass Network stood fast, though. "I had a job to do," shrugs Eckes. "And [the Grave Rave incident] was perfect for me. It was a way to prove my company. I was not going to let anything stop me."

Drop Bass was obsessively careful in the planning and positioning of its parties, often holding them outside city limits. Between the winter of 1992 and the winter of 1994, Drop Bass threw sixteen large-scale raves. One fifteen-hundred-to-two-thousand head event came off approximately every three weeks, and not one got shut down. The music Drop Bass promoted was extremely hard acid and jackhammering gabba techno, mainly from Germany and the Lowlands, as played by an expanding Midwest network of tough-as-hell DJs: Woody McBride, also known as DJ ESP, from Minneapolis; Delta 9, Astrocat, and

Hyperactive from Chicago; Mr. Bill and Acid Boy Todd P from Milwaukee; Terry Mullan from St. Louis, Missouri (who subsequently became one of America's better-known progressive-house DJs). At one party, in an "effort" to quell the complaints of some ravers who thought Drop Bass raves should include a bit of house — or something less than 170 BPM — Eckes partitioned the room with tall hay-bale dividers, which acted as a sound barrier. He put one little-known Midwest house DJ (DJ Davey Dave) on one side and a herd of slamming hardcore DJs on the other. "The sound system on the hardcore side was twice as loud," giggles Eckes, "effectively drowning out the house. We were trying to prove a point. I guess it was pretty immature."

Drop Bass Network was legendary for its masses of sound, because Eckes had used Storm Rave as a blueprint. Woody McBride had put together a Storm-worthy wall of sound in Minneapolis, which he would cart off to Drop Bass parties. Kids called it "Woody's Wall of Sound." They still talk about how clear the bass was. "I had fifty bass bins," explains McBride — "manifold boxes with eighteen-inch subwoofers and a rock-scene techie." Soon, he continues, walls like this were in demand among Midwest ravers as a party essential; flyers would advertise speaker stacks as prominently as they'd promote DJs. "Yeah, 'one hundred thousand watts of trouser-ruffling bass!' — that kinda thing. A lot of the mystique was visual: nobody really needs that much sound. The wall took on some big meaning. It became the center of a spiritual, communal experience — people dancing right up to it, people hugging the speakers, sticking their heads in bins, just totally enveloped in hard-beating, pounding bass. It was gorgeous."

Eckes set up appropriately hard atmospheres for his speaker-hugging ravers. He remembers one Drop Bass rave for which the venue was a "burned-out building with holes in the floors, in the process of being sandblasted." There was debris everywhere, and before the party they swept the rubble into a pile. "I guess to some ravers it looked like a sandbox. By the middle of the night there were tons of them playing in this heap of asbestos, fiberglass, and broken glass. That was a really crazy night. There was a big, bloody fight because of gang-bangers. We liked having gang-bangers at the parties because it gave this rough-and-tough atmosphere we wanted."

Drop Bass punters would swallow multiple tabs — sometimes quarter-sheets — of acid, ignorant of, or simply against, the huggable-snugglable E. Eckes admits that he may have "had a hand" in this ascendance of LSD. "The music — the distortion of hardcore and gabba techno — just fit with LSD so well," he says. "We encouraged everyone to take acid and fought extremely hard not to let E into the scene. We wanted acid to define Milwaukee's rave culture more than anything. Ecstasy, and all the happy songs and stupid talk that came with it, were irrelevant to us."

The 1993–94 DBN flyers are a treasure trove of peak-era Drop Bassian rave ideology. Eckes would always include phrases like, "demons of the darkside taking control of your soul," using fonts so Gothic-ly serifed as to be almost illegible. Parties were called "Ascension" and "Psychosis" and "Hellbent" and "Grave Reverence" (a year after the Grave Rave police bust; "We can't take credit for last year's legendary Grave event," reads the sarcastic flyer, "but we can for this one"). Soon Drop Bass had started describing its events as "techno-pagan rituals" instead of raves. By this point, DBN ravers had developed a casual interest in the writings of Anton LaVey, who, in 1966, founded the Church of Satan, the notorious wing of Satanism sometimes referred to by rockers like Rob Zombie, Marilyn Manson, and, before them, Ozzy Osbourne. Ravers took what they needed from the Church of Satan's library ("indulgence instead of abstinence!"), and ignored the unravey bits ("It is un-Satanic to cloud your brain and impair your judgment with mind-altering substances"). They confused Satanism with Ozzyland heavy-metalism, saluting each other with the sign of the Beast, wearing badges that proclaimed, "I love death metal" or "Last night the Devil saved my life," and tossing the word "extreme" around a lot. There was even a faction known for its "hair swinging": rocker longhairs who would stand in the back of the room and sling their locks around in time to the music.

As did the organizers of San Francisco's Come-Unity parties, Drop Bass used Xeroxed pamphlets and little information flyers as the medium for their message. "Our propaganda process," explains Eckes. "We did all these flyers that we'd give out [at parties], just like basic advertisements for hell and stuff, promoting the Devil." One of Eckes's favorite handouts featured the words of Das Energy's Paul Williams and was titled *Hell, Satan, Drop Bass Network*:

> . . . There is no such thing as evil.
> The concept of evil is a crutch.
> We will not heal until we toss away the crutch.
> . . . Stop chasing your tail. Embrace your Self.
> Lucifer returns to Heaven!
> Let there be dancing in the streets.
> The only sin is self-hatred
> We call it sin but its true name is Delusion.
> We have got to get back to the Garden.
> Easily done.
> We are *in* the Garden.
> Let us open our eyes.

In a strange way, Satanism was an ideal religion for the American raver. In Europe, a good part of the earlier ethos of rave had to do with people dropping themselves into a mass, getting lost in the crowd, giving up their personal identity for a much stronger group identity. When rave reached America, though, this idea was gradually lost, beaten down by the all-American Gap/ CK cult of be-yourself-be-original-be-different. "I think here rave was thought to be more about being an oddity, a freak," says Eckes. It was about being eye-catching: you weren't a drop in the bucket — you were more like a drop on a flat canvas, clustered with thousands of other drops, all with slightly different shapes.

There is an intrinsic irony in joining a group as means of individualizing yourself. How can you be part of a herd without blending in, without being herded? The Church of Satan has some nifty answers to that question. Although you have to join the Church of Satan, among that institution's venal sins (bad sins, not good sins) is "herd conformity: only fools follow along with the herd." "The key," Church of Satan high priestess Blanche Barton once wrote, "is to choose a master wisely instead of being enslaved by the whims of many."

◆

Kurt Eckes was, without a doubt, the "wisely chosen master" of Milwaukee/Midwest rave. He is still the only rave promoter to speak of in Milwaukee and the only promoter in the Midwest capable of drawing in the whole of the Midwest circuit, which began fracturing in the mid-nineties. In 1993, along with Patrick Spencer and Woody McBride, Eckes set up Drop Bass Records (both Spencer and McBride have since left the label). Drop Bass, with its "cute skull" logo, "Midwest Hardcorps" school of producers, and tracks like Delta 9's "Deep 13" or McBride's "Bad Acid — No Such Thing," immediately found much acclaim in European hardcore territory. The label was a piece of underground marketing perfection. It had a fantastically crafted Web site, adhered strictly to certain recognizable logos and typefaces, and offered merchandise — like the popular "Hear no evil, see no evil, speak no evil — *live evil!*" T-shirt. The official colors of the Drop Bass labels, used on everything from record sleeves to T-shirts, were red, black, and white.

"The colors of the Fascist flag," says Eckes. "I found the combination aesthetically pleasing." In college, Eckes had minored in history as he worked towards his engineering degree. It was during this period that his interest in Nazism was piqued. "Look, I do take pride in my German lineage, and I won't block out big chunks of history. So, I thought, even though I've been taught to believe the Nazis were fucked-up people, they still had the best-dressed soldiers and the best imagery, the best rallies and the best architecture. Everything about the Nazis looked incredible. Visually, even the swastika appealed to me. I realized it worked. Nazi imagery worked. The Devil stuff had worked in the Midwest, so I figured this might be the next step in terms of just filling people up with extreme imagery. I pushed the [Fascist] aesthetic as far as I could on flyers, record sleeves, logos. . . . Some kids hated taking flyers from us, but no promoter dared come up against us, so people *had* to take flyers from us."

By the mid-nineties, the worst-kept secret in techno was that gabba-hardcore had become the sound of certain sections of Germany's New Right. It was being played at neo-Nazi rallies and extolled by right-wing youth leaders as "pure," indigenous music. Yet the king of Milwaukee's scene says he was not down with that; he claims he is not a Fascist. He says that much like his "total hero," Marilyn Manson, he is "just into getting a rise out of people so that they will react and start thinking." I mostly believe him — although it would also be reasonable not to believe a word he says.

It's unclear whether Milwaukee ravers began to think that Eckes had gone too far or whether the increasing availability of foreign DJ-culture magazines like *Mixmag* and *Muzik*, as well as burgeoning American versions like *Urb* and *XLR8R*, opened kids' eyes to other forms of dance music besides gabba and German-style hardcore. But, by 1994, while Drop Bass Records was finding success in Europe, most gabba and hardcore stopped selling well at the three Milwaukee record shops. Established local DJs toned it down by turning to hard acid, and budding spinners turned to Relief Records-style 1990s Chicago house or breaks or Detroit techno instead.

An incredibly keen businessman, Eckes began rethinking his "only hardcore" party-making strategy. In 1994, he arranged to meet a friend, *Reactor* magazine editor David Prince, in a coffee shop. Eckes had just finished reading Tom Wolfe's *Electric Kool-Aid Acid Test*, the kaleidoscopic account of a cross-country trip that acid crusader Ken Kesey and his Merry Pranksters took in a painted bus. Eckes says the book "struck [him] with an epiphany." "I was, like, 'Oh, wait a second. I take acid every day, and here are some people from the sixties who took it every day twice, and they are still living, and they had a really good time.' That whole, 'on the bus, taking things further' concept — it clicked. It related to everything I'd always thought the rave scene should be about. David Prince and I thought it would be cool to do something along those lines — going places no one's ever been." They began planning a three-day rave camp out.

This first Furthur event ("Furthur" was the word on the sign fronting Kesey's adventure-bound bus) took place from April 29 to May 1, 1994, on an expanse of farmland in Hixton, Wisconsin. In his book *Energy Flash*, Simon Reynolds describes David Prince and DBN's techno-pagan camp out as "a lawless zone." Tommie Sunshine describes it as "a place where there was just no reason to stop." It was Eckes's ultimate vision of decadence and hedonism expanded, yet softened to attract all of the growing Midwest rave sector — there was nothing about the Devil, and no Nazi-tinged graphics were used on the psychedelic poster-style flyer, which (almost nauseatingly) reads, "a gathering celebrating the flowering of our summer and our culture. . . . Three days of blissful enlightenment." House and techno and drum & bass and ambient DJs were fully represented; Ecstasy was available. From the outside, the party may have seemed completely un-Kurt Eckes, a bit hippy-dippy. There was a conglomeration of the smashed VW buses and RVs you'd normally see at a Grateful Dead concert. There was also plenty of parking-lot age-of-love mysticism and tie-dyed dance-around-a-bonfire paganism (instead of the usual fuck-your-mother

Devilism). Teenaged "soft ravers" came from as far away as Kentucky intoning their fave buzzword, "PLUR" (Peace, Love, Unity, Respect). Still, from the inside, the party was pure Drop Bass.

Tommie Sunshine had decided that Furthur was to be his last rave ever. He had been traveling for four years, "showing up in polyester suits with a hot chick on each arm" at every type of rave imaginable. He always got in for free and never paid for his drugs; he had "major status — the destructive kind." And he just couldn't do it anymore. He felt depressed, burned. He had been telling people for months before the event that he was either going to OD at Furthur or — if he made it through the three days — move to Atlanta "to start [his] life over." "I had seriously cast my fate to the gods," he says. But why, over all others, was this the determining party? "Because this was *Furthur*. And, after it, things were never, ever, going to be the same. It would have been like dying at Woodstock. That's what this party was: the Woodstock of the Midwest, the best party and the last party."

The list of twenty DJs at the 1994 Furthur included the Hardkisses, Spenser Kinsey, Barry Weaver, Frankie Bones, Adam X, Nigel Richards, and Diesel Boy; there was an Aphex Twin live show and a host of Midwest regulars. The list of drugs Tommie ingested from the time he arrived in his Monster Truck T-shirt and best polyester tracksuit is much longer: "seven hits of E, twenty hits of acid — I took them regularly, in halves — a zillion amphetamines and downers washed down with Jack Daniels. I was smoking opium, hash, or pot every five minutes for the entire three days. I never slept (no one did), didn't eat a thing. Water was hard to find — I didn't drink anything but alcohol. At one point, I sat in a tent for three hours with a tank of nitrous."

By Saturday, the second night of Furthur, Tommie's clothes were completely caked with mud. Exhausted, no longer even able to remember what hunger felt like, he traipsed up and down the mudslide hills of springtime Hixton in complete darkness (DBN was not known for its lighting), searching for water, friends, a different tent to hang in. "It was fucking *Lord of the Flies*," he recalls. "I simply couldn't believe this whole thing was *allowed*, that a lightning bolt from God didn't crash down on the Furthur site, it was so decadent." In America, the ravers are young, usually under twenty-one. These young revelers rolled in the mud flaked on acid mixed with E, nitrous, meth, K; they hung from trees yelling incoherently; they stood nude in front of fires "for no apparent reason," sharing drugs and having sex and dancing like maniacs with people they had just met. Furthur truly was "a lawless zone."

"That night, Saturday, the second night, was the most powerful night I had ever experienced," says Sunshine. "There were no lights in the main tent. We were in pitch darkness, only lit by one laser and some kids who had flashlights, in the middle of nowhere." His friends were worried about him. "They were watching me dance. I had gotten to the point where my body wouldn't stop the knee-jerk reaction of dancing, but I looked like I was in agony. Physically, I was in hell, but my body couldn't rest because I was so pumped up on drugs. They had to drag me off the dance floor and put me to sleep in the car. They watched me try to sleep for five hours and they wouldn't leave my side because, at five-second intervals, I would laugh, I would cry, I would thrash around. It was a complete spiritual-sensory freak-out. It was like I was possessed. We were all basically dancing to the apocalypse at that point. If anybody had brought a video camera to Furthur, it would have exploded."

◆

Furthur, population four thousand, status still completely illegal, celebrated its four-year anniversary in 1998. It has proven itself one of the most durable rave events in the whole of America, and Drop Bass Network has proven itself one of the country's most resilient promotions group. Kurt Eckes, who still lives in a Milwaukee warehouse — only now with a wife and two

Porsches ("my babies") — says he feels he got "his message across" through the events he staged. Yet he sees them as separate from his "hardcore musical vision," which remains the vision of his record labels. "The future of hardcore," he says, "is in taking it out of the rave scene, more into the experimental-rock direction." He name-checks German DJ/producer Alec Empire as a kind of mentor. In the early nineties, Empire, a German Jew who, like Eckes, often uses Nazi imagery for effect, removed himself from what he called "the apathy and empty ideologies of Germany's rave scene." He then initiated a genre titled "digital hardcore," a consolidation of punkish live shows, hollering politicized vocals, winging guitars, and pummeling gabba-hardcore beats. His band, Atari Teenage Riot, has had much success on the American indie-rock circuit. Following the road paved by Empire and ATR (among others), Eckes has lately been pursuing a "noisier, nondance" direction with his DBN sublabel, Ghetto Safari: "I think in order for it to be allowed to go further, it has to stop being seen as party music or dance music, because, at least from my experience, you just reach a ceiling in the party [context] — like people saying, 'Hey, this isn't fun anymore.'"

The Milwaukee scene essentially revolves around Furthur now. Drop Bass concentrates on the one event, and there are very few raves besides. A hardcore techno scene does exist in America but Milwaukee is far from being its capital. "I guess the city has suffered since Drop Bass stopped doing regular parties," says Eckes. "Nobody has taken our place, and the city is dead again." As their counterparts do in lots of other American rave cities circa 1998, Milwaukee kids say their scene is "pretty over." There is lots of talk of the golden years of the earlier nineties when Milwaukee ruled the Midwest. Tommie Sunshine thinks maybe he should write a book about it — put it all down on paper lest he forget anything. He now works consulting and managing bands and house producers like the Wamdue Kids — in Atlanta.

5 ORLANDO
Killer Drugs, "Gangster Ravers," and
the Florida Funky Breaks Sound

Orlando is a city so purpose-built it's almost surreal. Before Walt Disney World was completed a few miles outside of it in 1971, Orlando was just a broiling Central Florida ghost town, a tiny, out-of-the-way nub of commercial nothingness. Within a decade, it had metamorphosed into a clean grid of seemingly endless for-your-convenience parking lots — vast sections of paved terrain with new, square buildings stuck in the middle of them: hotels, motels, malls, fast-food huts, emporiums, family restaurants, gas station/minimart complexes, and discount outlets like "The Largest Athletic Shoe Outlet in the World!" This city, which is intersected every which way by four-lane highways, can at times seem like nothing more than a giant food/gas/lodging rest stop. There are barely any sidewalks in Orlando. There are many "drive-thrus," though: drive-thru drugstores, drive-thru liquor stores, drive-thru supermarket car-order mazes. In order to use a bank machine — all drive-thru — the rare person who does not drive (me) is forced to stand in a lineup of cars. The city is constructed to cater to the whims of holidaymakers. Why force these people to step out of their air-conditioned Budget rental cars? It's 120 degrees outside, and, anyway, they haven't come to Orlando to see the city. They're only passing the night before they go off to have their picture taken with Mickey bright and early the next morning.

The city is a haven for the nouveau: there's no peeling paint here despite the blistering heat. The most aged building is sixty years old. A sign means neon. Antique is a style. Sophistication is drinking "frozen double-latte tallboys" instead of plain coffee. Even the major industries — aerospace, electronics, and theme-park tourism (not only Disney holds sway here now, but also Busch Gardens, Sea World, Universal Studios, MGM-Disney Studios, and so on) — are new and young. One wonders how anybody could establish roots in a spot already so devoid of roots, how one could grow old in such a juvenile environment. In truth, not many have yet. In terms of population, Orlando is the exact opposite of the better-established Miami/Fort Lauderdale area, which boasts the largest concentration of elderly people in the United States. Orlando is a youthful city, where the twenty-four-and-under age bracket is the most significant segment of the population (over 33 percent in 1996 — a considerable jump from the American overall figure of 29 percent).

This has made Orlando a place where rave could spark, glow, and subsequently burn. "If you are telling the story of Orlando rave," says DJ Icey, the most famed DJ to come out of the Orlando scene, "you are telling the story of the rise and the fall. And that fall was harsher than anywhere else in the US." Some Orlando doctors estimate that there were almost sixty drug-related deaths in Orlando — by no means a large city — between 1991 and 1997, and they link most of those deaths to the club and rave scenes. Bad Ecstasy and the mixing of the sedative GHB (gamma-hydroxy butyrate) with other substances seem to have been the main culprits; however, several DJs and club owners I spoke with also alluded to heroin use, or even "a heroin problem," within the rave scene in the mid-nineties. The Orlando police and government officials set up a Rave Review Task Force in 1997 and imposed a curfew on clubs (where all Orlando raves are held), completely stifling any after-hours activity. They proposed holding club owners partly responsible for any drug-related incidents within a certain radius of their establishments. And, at one point, they even tested out an ordinance that prohibited people under the age of eighteen from being out after midnight. All this pushed rave promoters beyond the city limits. It did not completely kill Orlando rave, for rave still exists in the area, but it certainly knocked a good bit of life out of the city's rave scene, which, in the mid-nineties, was one of North America's most vibrant, populated, and surprisingly creative.

✦

I say "creative," mainly because of the original Floridian rave sound, funky breaks, said to have been initiated by the enigmatic DJ Icey and his Zone imprint. Floridian funky breaks, an uptempo breakbeat-house style that owes a small debt to early British breakbeat-hardcore and a large debt to the booming, electro-fied Floridian party-rap style of Miami bass, has been the only dance genre entirely created within the American rave scene. The style did not infiltrate Europe to any impressive degree, but it did establish itself in many American rave cities, notably on the West Coast, through popular California DJs DJ Dan and John Howard (who maintains that funky breaks was born in the Bay Area and is more the product of the Hardkiss Brothers than of anyone in Florida) as well as the LA label City of Angels.

Much like British hardcore was in early-nineties England, funky breaks has often been denigrated as a simplistic, "cheap" kind of music by American dance cognoscenti. Those cognoscenti living in Orlando derogatively call breaks fans "gangster ravers," or sometimes even "White-trash ravers." (The breaks scene in Orlando is majority White, but it is yards more multicultural than the rest of the rave/house scene; it's also predominantly middle class, so the "White trash" tag seems a bit misplaced.) The denigrators consider the sound to be something for kids who want easy thrills or who don't know any better. In a certain way, the sound *is* simplistic, relying as it does on a booming car-stereo-worthy bass line, a looped breakbeat, one or two rap/electro/scratch samples, a squidgy 303 buildup somewhere in the middle of every track, and a sunshiney feel. This is not thinking-man's dance music. Yet to me, funky breaks has always seemed like one of the more exciting developments in North American rave, partly because it is a domestic style, but mainly because of its homegrown cultural adjuncts — namely, bits of hip-hop culture.

The first funky-breaks DJ I ever heard was named Rob Brown. In 1993, he was living in my hometown of Montreal, Canada. Brown was so incredibly white-bread suburban that people called him "Downtown Rob Brown" because he absolutely *wasn't*. He was not considered as important as the DJs who played techno or "quality" house, and he was usually relegated to DJing the backrooms at raves. The interesting thing about Brown's funky breaks is that they glued together a multicultural posse that would follow him to every gig — hip-hop boys, who, in 1993, were not your typical raves patrons, at least not in Montreal. Rob Brown's crowd went to both rap concerts and raves. They looked ghetto: gold chains, saggy jeans with one leg rolled up, cocked baseball caps. Some of them were graffiti taggers and carried spray cans in their backpacks. When most DJs were on, these boys just skulked in the corner. When Brown was on, they break danced.

In 1993, it wasn't rare to spot a pack of kids doing body pops and worms and half-baked back spins on the floor at North American raves. It seemed a natural progression from the robot-making-boxes shuffle that had become the absolute American rave dance by then. But these movements never seemed any-thing more than dance-floor tricks. With the advent of funky breaks, break dancing in rave was given a sound, and a little subculture gelled, one that bridged hip-hop and house. It wasn't the first time someone had tried combining hip-hop and dancy-

pants clubland. In late-eighties Chicago, producers like Fast
Eddie and Tyree Cooper introduced an ill-fated composite style
called "hip-house," which had rappers throwing down lyrics
over house's 4–4 beat. Chicago hip-house fizzled after about a
dozen records. "Funky breaks is different," says DJ Icey, "coz it's
not just the two things stuck together for the hell of it. It's more
the natural [out]growth of lots of rave kids in the USA growing
up with hip-hop. Remember, these are kids who were born in
the eighties and [formed] their taste in the nineties, and in the
US the nineties have been all about hip-hop."

Orlando funky breakers readily cite their music's connection
to hip-hop in general and hip-hop's "old school" in particular.
They are less inclined to associate funky breaks in any way,
shape, or form with their genre's most obvious influence: Miami
bass — the bass-drenched Floridian style of ghetto hip-hop
whose nucleus is bastardized 1980s electro and whose most
famous luminaries are 2 Live Crew. "Miami bass?" exclaims
Orlando breaks DJ Spice. "That's *booty* music, man. Not the same
thing at all." The staple Miami-bass video image is one of big-
backed women doing the jiggy wind in Lycra hot pants with their
asses in a rapper's face. The genre's lyrics are notoriously dirty in
an elementary-school kind of way, and there's lots of swearing.
This is the kind of music that macho boardwalk-cruisers soup
up their lowrider stereos for. It's not a respected style — it's considered "trash." You could say that in terms of reputation it is to
hip-hop what handbag is to house.

Yet, T&A lyrics aside, funky breaks and Miami bass can
sound identical at points: booty bass, electro blips and breaks;
happy, boiling, jump-up, rump-shaking, unpretentious *partay*
music. You hear lots of Miami bass in Florida, and some Orlando
breaks DJs, like D-Xtreme, even began their careers playing the
stuff. So why would association be denied? "Attaching breaks to
the most disrespected kind of hip-hop in existence — this em-
barrassing booty music half of Florida is seemingly trying to live

down — I guess is not something people here want to do," says Charlie Londono of Florida breaks label Just Funkin'. "Lots of people already think funky breaks are [unsophisticated], and people into breaks may think the [Miami] bass connection would only make things worse. What it comes down to at the end is racism — musical racism. Some people are just afraid of party music."

◆

One of the coolest things about rave in America is that it did something to displace the original big-city seats of power in US dance music and democratized things to the extent that places like Milwaukee, Portland, Baltimore, or Orlando could become important. At the beginning of the nineties, Orlando rave had a buzz on it. Rave kids were moving there from other parts of Florida, often taking daytime theme-park jobs to support their lifestyle. And even some DJs and promoters came from places as diverse as Virginia, New York State, Boston, and Canada. This migration, coupled with a few magazine articles, weekly events in the thousands, and a lot of word of mouth, was building Orlando a solid rep in the kingdom of the glo-stick.

The beginnings of Orlando rave can be traced to a club called Oz, or, as the locals say it, "Aaahz." As were rave centers in many other American cities, Oz was sparked not by 1986 Chicago house, but by Ecstasy and the British acid-house wave. Year zero was 1988, the look was overalls/whistles/smileys, the site was a cheesy "old" theater called the Beechem (later called Dekko's), the night was Saturday. The promoter of Oz, a ballsy, sexy broad named Stace Bass, would get on the microphone at the end of every Saturday night to make inspirational announcements ("We are one!"). The DJs were Kimball Collins, a name still synonymous with Orlando house, and Dave Canalte, who now is the musical director at a Disney-owned nightlife concept called Pleasure Island — he plays at a club that has a waterfall inside it.

The stories spun about Oz are as beautiful and hazy as a smoke-machine mist, but they're nothing you haven't heard before in the context of first-time E users: a ring of clasped hands circling the dance floor, all-out euphoria, two thousand people leaving the club at 10 A.M. en route to small parties in private houses that would soon turn into weekender communes, drug-induced love found in new and interesting places.

Oz set the tone for what would become a notable characteristic of Orlandonian rave-music taste: easy and uplifting, not severe or aggressive. "It's a happy-happy town," says DJ Dave Canalte. "Not a hard town. Orlando is soft. People are nice. You have to remember that tons of the kids in this town work at the theme parks or in the service industry. It's hard to shake off that smile after work, I guess." Canalte is right: happy is everywhere in Orlando. Images of happy faces grace storefronts and rental cars and restaurant menus; waiters are so happy to bring you a stack of griddle cakes or refill your "bottomless" soft drink that they seem in danger of exploding from sheer pleasure.

At Sub-Zero, a Tuesday-nighter less than half a mile away in a venue that usually played host to country-rock bands, another aspect of Orlando's sound was developing through the efforts of resident DJ Eddie Pappas, better known as DJ Icey: the preoccupation with breakbeats. Icey was known to be a bit of a weird-cake — a mysterious and tremendously moody man from St. Augustine, Florida, who kept to himself. His nickname was Icey not because he was ghetto, or because his club's name was Sub-Zero, but because he kept his apartment so cold it was inhospitable. "I love air-conditioning," says Icey. "It's too hot here. Cold. It's my thing." Icey's other "thing" was hip-hop instrumentals mixed with Chicago hip-house and certain break-beat-house records coming out of England at the turn of the nineties. His favorite UK labels were Ozone and D-Zone, two small imprints that specialized in mid-tempo, peppy breaks (Icey eventually named his own label Zone in homage). "I found that people here enjoyed dancing to a nonstraight beat," says Icey. "Breakbeats didn't have the monotony of the straight kick [that standard house has]. Breaks always have a different snare and kick pattern, and when you listen to breaks, you nod your head, tap your foot, and the next thing you know you are dancing. I can't believe everyone doesn't play them. There is something magical about how they get people moving."

In 1991, the owners of an Orlando oyster bar called Calico Jack's phoned Icey. They were about to open a barnlike night-club that they needed over five thousand patrons to fill. The club was called the Edge, and it was a franchise in a chain of Edges that usually worked within a Top-40 format. Also enlisted was Robbie Clarke, a house DJ who had just opened a record shop in Orlando called Underground Records Source. "I think it was a mistake," says Icey. "The Calico Jack's guys didn't know what they were doing and just figured a DJ is a DJ. Maybe they thought we played Top 40 — who knows?"

The "mistake" of these oyster-bar owners turned out to be a smash success on many levels. For five years, from 1991 to 1996, five to ten thousand patrons passed through the Edge to hear Icey play almost every Saturday night. That's an average of almost half a million Saturday patrons a year. The Edge is the club that put Orlando on the rave map; it's where the funky-breaks sound/culture gelled. A fresh school of DJ/producers would soon come out of the breaktastic ether: DJ Spice, DJ Friction, Baby Anne, DJ Sandy, D-Xtreme, Mike & Charlie, Stylus, AK 1200 (now one of America's better-known drum & bass DJs), Atom, Jefee, DJ Security, and Cliff T. Graduates from Oz frequented the Edge, but, more importantly, it was also the place where the newer ravers, soon dubbed "Edge Kids" really got it together. They were the ones who manifested Adidas stripes, graffiti tags, phat pants, multiple tattoos, monstrous piercings, and floor spins. "Some people were break dancing before the Edge," says

Icey. "There was definitely that style, but I think my breaks accelerated the trend in Orlando. Especially for girls. Girls liked my music a lot because it's easy and it's funky. I mean, um, it's dance music of the danciest kind.

In 1993, when the Edge was in full (head) spin, Icey set up his funky breaks label Zone, which soon lead to an endless string of other Orlando-area breaks labels, including Kram, Just Funkin', DB, Knight Life, MAFDAP, and Fade. "My first record was called *Energy Tracks Volume I.* I made the record so that I would have something new to play in clubs," says Icey. "By 1993, there were no records available in the genre that I liked. England was all fast hardcore by then, and those crazy hardcore BPM did not suit Orlando. *Energy Tracks* was supersimple, just a midtempo breakbeat and a coupla samples, but it worked." Icey's style has not changed tremendously since 1993. Neither has his quick-fix music-making philosophy. "Since *Energy Tracks*, I have pretty much put out a record a month. I don't spend a lot of time making my tracks. I just go in and I try to bang it out in a day. Some of the tracks show that they were made that quickly, too. But it's just a spontaneous thing for me. And I try to keep it that way. Why complicate things?"

The music that fueled the Edge may be uncomplicated, but the legacy of the club is anything but. While in Orlando, I was taken to a progressive house club called Icon, which looked like it was decorated in the heyday of 1980s chunky-industrio chic, but was actually decorated in 1997. There was a dress code that deemed people had to wear collars (no crewneck T-shirts), and no backpacks were allowed. My hosts — two local DJs, named Daisy and Susanna — considered this side of Orlando the "most international," the most appropriate to feature in a book. I asked Daisy where the anti-T-shirt/backpack rule had come from. She replied that without it, Icon "would turn into the Edge all over again. Here they wanna keep out those trash gangster ravers —

those kids, those children, the break dancers. There is no break dancing here, of course. We can't have anything like the Edge happening here again."

There is something of a conspiracy of silence about the Edge in Orlando. Even Icey only mentioned the place two or three times in interview. "Because the Edge is the club that took Orlando over the edge," says Orlando promoter Eli Tobias, who hosts a weekly break-dancing contest. "It was dirty."

The dirt was, of course, drugs. The Edge opened up a new drug culture in Orlando, complete with new rituals and even a new lingo: you didn't take drugs at the Edge, you "ate" them. Bad drugs made you "ate up," powerful drugs made you "blow up." The most defining drug in the era of the Edge was the pills the kids called "Wafers." Wafers were one of those mélanges sold as Ecstasy that may actually have contained no MDMA whatsoever. These pills first arrived in 1992, bearing the street name Texas Tallboys because of their strangely large size and because they were said to have emanated from a circle of Texas dealers who had begun working into Orlando. They'd heard about the city's highly active rave environment. Wafers were particularly influential, because in a town the size of Orlando, when there is one kind of E going around, there is just one kind of E going around. Wafers were the thing on the street for just over two years — an extremely long time for an Ecstasy "brand."

"They were what you could get. For the longest time. They were these big, huge, nasty pills the size of a quarter," says Chris Hand, owner of Orlando breaks label Knight Life. "Wafers would make you throw up within fifteen minutes after eating one. I mean, like, bad, bad — blowing the fuck up, puking like crazy. You'd be high for twelve hours on one of those." Hand believes that Wafers were composed of "bad pill powder" held together by melted fertilizer. Orlando breaks DJ Spice thinks Wafers were "sick shit glued together with some kinda bathroom cleaner, or CarBondo, that stuff you repair cars with." He liked them. "You could take half of one and blow the fuck up. They were that strong. The half would get you totally *out*."

But — based on the fact that you would vomit like mad after ingesting a Wafer, then zone out into slow-motion territory, fall into yourself, and feel timelessly strung out and extremely high, to the point of not being able to speak — some people in Orlando began thinking that Wafers contained heroin. "People would see these brown specs in Wafers and think brown equals heroin," says DJ AK1200. "There were these 'chocolate chip' Wafers at the Edge, which were just loaded with brown dots and were particularly nasty. Everybody thought those were H for sure. . . ." But heroin was an unlikely additive. "I have never come across any sort of Ecstasy which contained heroin," says Push, coauthor of *On E: A Book about Ecstasy*. "No dealer would cut E with something so much more expensive."

Wafers are long gone, along with all concrete evidence as to their makeup. Some of their effects seem to have been similar to those of a pseudo-Ecstasy called "Snowballs," which were popular in England around 1992. Snowballs were also large pills. They contained no MDMA, but they packed a huge dose of MDA, a relative of MDMA with a much harsher "zone out" comedown. Anyway, whatever the composition of Wafers, their effects were widespread. Just as amphetamine-sold-as-Ecstasy was one of the prime reasons British hardcore began its climb up the BPM ladder, Wafers may have had a hand in creating the slower, midtempo breaks sound. At the Edge, before the real proliferation of "pure" funky-breaks records, Icey would often play British hardcore records. "But he pitched them down! To about 120 BPMs," says AK1200. "Some of them would have had to be pitched down to minus 8, or played on 33, because they were so fast: 120 [BPMs] — that became the Orlando tempo. It was all people could stand . . . they were just on too many sit-down Es, too many weirdo drugs."

The stories of anything-goes drug experimentation at the

Edge sometimes sound like the kind of party escapades you'd hear about in junior high: that some kids tried smoking pine needles or inhaling a bathroom air freshener or Krazy Glue in order to get wasted. At the Edge, kids were interested in anything that might alter their state. Besides the expensive intoxicants like Wafers or other sorts of Ecstasy, or the standard sides of spliff, booze, acid, and some cocaine, Edge kids were experimenting with all sorts of sedatives, Ephedrine, fly-by-night concoctions, and even Robitussin, a cough syrup that makes for a hallucinogenic holiday if you drink half a bottle. Most mornings at the Edge, the floor would be littered with "whip-its" — nitrous-oxide cartridges, the little silver oblongs made for whipped-cream dispensers, which kids would break open and inhale for a twenty-second high.

Heroin has never been considered a rave drug. But, by 1994, three years into the Edge, after the club had started to be known as the spot for an increasingly famous Icey and an increasingly ate-up crew of what were increasingly being tagged "gangster ravers," heroin began appearing. Orlando DJ AK1200 hypothesizes that kids were more open to heroin at the Edge because they believed that they had already tried the stuff in Wafer form.

Florida has traditionally been a central import state for South American, Central American, Caribbean, and Mexican drugs. "But this heroin problem was new, in that it was popping up in new places," says John Marsa, ex-owner of Orlando club the Firestone, who has become something of a political lobbyist and drug activist. The Orlando rave scene, circa the mid-nineties, was not the only new place heroin was popping up. The proportion of American twelfth-graders who had used heroin doubled between 1990 and 1996 (from .9 percent to 1.8 percent). "Heroin became a nose drug — that's how it reached these kids," explains Marsa. "In the late eighties, these very intelligent Colombian cartel operators were beginning to grow poppies in South America ... they began purifying their yield to a degree where it was so strong people could use less. People didn't have to inject it any-more for a big buzz. And, with the purification of heroin — making it a nose drug — they developed a whole new, young, hip market of heroin users. All based on the fact that the stigma of needles was gone. People figured heroin was less addictive when snorted rather than shot up — which is bullshit — but, anyway, they started buying in."

Due to the polydrug habits of Edge kids, ambulances were called to the club more and more often. "Oh yeah, it was, like, watch 'em drop," says Orlando progressive-house DJ Andy Hughes. "At points, it seemed like there was someone dying every two weeks. It got to the point where it was, like, 'Oh, you know so-and-so. Yeah, he dropped this Saturday.' It wasn't any big-scene people, like any of the important DJs, though, just kids."

The degree to which Orlando became desensitized to these drug casualties is astounding. One high-school student tells me the story, possibly a legend, of a teen who was discovered dead in the downtown Travelodge, where groups of rave kids used to take out rooms on big party nights. The surreally cheery motel was such a popular hangout that, in 1996, a raver had blacked out the first letter on the hotel's sign with spray paint, making it read "ravelodge." "They were partyin' around this kid, doing drugs, and he was dead. Partying around a fuckin' corpse," says the high-school student, who wishes not to be named. "They left him in the hotel room covered in drug [paraphernalia] and went out raving anyway. The kid was found much later."

Everybody in the Orlando scene seems to have an Edge-era drug-death story, and most are prepared to tell it as if they were describing last night's episode of COPS. "I was at the Edge when one girl died," says DJ Spice. "I was outside when it happened, and I saw them carryin' her. It was, like, six or seven in the morning, and they were running with her, yellin' 'Get out of the way!' and she was, like, dead. I guess she just ODed like everyone else — maybe Wafers, maybe heroin. It was in the courtyard of the Edge; it was outside, some kids found her sitting in a corner. They couldn't wake her up. So someone got security. I don't know how long she was left like that, but she was already stiff when they were carryin' her. . . . I thought this other guy was gonna drop on us that night, too, coz he said he ate three Wafers at once. He didn't say it, coz he couldn't talk, but someone told me. He was laying on the ground, right after that other girl died, with two girls holding him; his lips were blue, and he was, like, just shakin'. I was just, like, 'Time to go home.' Had enough for one night."

◆

A backlash was inevitable. The first sign of it came from within the scene itself. The resemblance between the split that would happen in Orlando towards the end of the Edge is remarkably similar to the split that occurred in England when rave began going hardcore bonkers. In England, the people who had been around in the early days, maybe people who had gone to Danny Rampling's Shoom or Paul Oakenfold's Spectrum, cattled out of rave once the scene had begun getting too young and too "common," too big and too messily drug-addled. They returned to clubgoing, started dressing up again, and began doing more "adult" drugs, like cocaine. They also began to uphold "classy" or "intelligent" forms of house and techno. The most notorious of these "higher" genres was progressive house: an overwrought, overthunk, overproduced, self-conscious, swooshy 'n swish style of British house music with a concentration on "musicality" over dance-floor practicality. Basically, prog was to house what prog was to rock: masturbatory; elitist. Progressive house, based around labels like Guerilla and acts like Leftfield, was an antirave genre, regularly described as "epic" or "oceanic" rather than "mental."

The people in Orlando who'd simply had it with the ambulances and druggy, break-dancing teens at the Edge followed England's lead and turned to progressive house as their clean getaway from the horrors of rave-gone-excessive. The Orlando heads who brought in prog and flew in UK progressive don DJ Sasha over fifteen times in a three-year period were the same people who were "there in the early days," much as the proglodites in the UK were. In Orlando's case, this old school comprised those who had gone to Oz. They, too, started dressing up (no backpacks, no sneakers, *collars*); they also sought out "less juvenile" drugs and patronized a new, expensively designed club called the Firestone, which had a "no break dancing" policy (if you did it, they would kick you out).

The club is referred to by those who run it as "the historic Firestone," because it is housed in a sixty-year-old building that used to be a Firestone Tires garage. It is an Orlando heritage building, one of the oldest in the city. The club opened in 1995, and its owner was John Marsa, of Miami. "Marsa was slick," says Oz's Stace Bass. "He had slick long hair, dressed like a casual slick guy. He just seemed rich, you know?" As the Firestone's resident DJ, Marsa hired Oz's old DJ — Kimball Collins, who, by then, was gaining fame outside Orlando for his smooth, progressive house sound. Marsa also hired a little, wiry, gingerheaded promo kid named Bevin O'Neil to help bring in a new after-hours crowd, which, until the Firestone, was the exclusive property of the Edge (the straights) and the smaller fringe clubs (the gays).

"We mixed gays and straights! *Gays* and *straights*," says Bevin O'Neil. "Nobody would have touched that idea in Orlando. Frat boys going home with drag queens by mistake! We were brilliant!" When O'Neil gets excited about something, his scratchy voice rises and rises until he is screaming at the top of his lungs. Everybody in Orlando seems to know him. He is usually described as a "character." He quotes President Kennedy and Charles Bukowski and British nightclub promoters like Dave Beer. He recites punk lyrics as if they were written by Wordsworth, and he'll shut his eyes at the end of his recitation and say, ruefully, "a true psalm for America, that is." He wanted to be a Beat poet. He'll tell you he's a genius. A visionary. A "born promoter." "Everyone hates me," he insists. "Everyone hates a success story."

"What I did, which was revolutionary," O'Neil wails, "was, not only did I infuse into the scene this gay/straight mix, but also I [introduced] the idea of an international hot spot. I'd have this big DJ from England play one week, that big DJ the next, and fly Sasha in to play the next. I opened Orlando up away from breaks and into clubbing sophistication."

The Edge began sliding in late 1995, and it would close in early 1996. But breaks kids were loath to visit the Firestone, a place that so clearly despised them and that they despised in return. A divide had opened up: straightbeat vs breakbeat, dressed-up vs ate-up, adult vs kid, mostly White vs multicultural, double-latte tallboys vs Texas Tallboys. Looking for floor space, breaks kids began frequenting a slew of smaller, skanky clubs, the only ones left that would accept break dancers. One such club was Ultra Violet.

"One night in 1996, I was booked at UV at the last minute, replacing some breaks DJ," says progressive-house DJ Remark. "I played some really quality progressive house music. I had come back from a trip and was really excited about my new records. But kids kept on coming up to the booth — like, 'What the hell is this garbage? Do ya have any Icey [records]? Anything funky? This shit sucks!' Even the girls were accosting me. Then, one by one, plop, plop, plop, they started sitting down on the dance floor, booing me and giving me the finger and the thumbs-down sign. So I was, like, 'Fuck them.' I dropped all the bass, pushed all the highs up, and sat there with my arms crossed. They all left the room. I'm only glad I wasn't hurt. These kids were so adamant about their music they were positively gang-like. Criminals! I could have been killed! I suppose low-class people like that don't like intelligent music."

"This is this kind of myth stuff which kept the Firestone up in its own [ivory] tower," says DJ AK1200 — "made them feel special." There is no evidence that breakers were (or are) any more "low class" than the two thousand or so prog-listening Firestone patrons. There was never even a concrete reason for the breakers to be dubbed "gangster ravers," either, besides a ghetto clothing style and a tendency to hang out in packs (they were teens, after all, and that's what teens do). "Man, these are just kids who think they are the shit and act all hard coz they're all into this hip-hop attitude thing," says AK1200. "They look in the mirror and go, 'Yeah!' — They've got the bog-chain wallet hangin' out and the big nasty JNKO's jeans [a popular American brand that makes extra-fat phat pants] and their backpacks. They'll get up and check chicks, y'know? Like, last time I was at a breaks club, I was with my girlfriend and she was wearing a dress and this guy walks by her sideways, tips his hat and goes, 'Yo.' Who takes that seriously here? I'm sure that kid's mom paid for his pants! I don't know about all this 'low class' stuff. Everybody in Orlando is comfortable enough — there really is no ghetto. Generally, Orlando is a safe place."

✦

Orlando does feel like a pretty safe place in terms of crime and violence. But something about the scene and the drugs has always forged a straight line to the hospital. For all its lofty intentions, the Firestone was soon flooded with drugs — not with Wafers, but with newer club drugs, in particular, one that was becoming very popular across the American rave-and-club scene. This drug was considered a good "older" alternative to Ecstasy; it was a sedative called GHB.

The first time I tried GHB (gamma-hydroxy butyrate) I was

convinced that it was the best drug on the planet — better than E, in certain ways. At twenty-five, I had a job and couldn't cope with the aftereffects of Ecstasy-fueled Saturdays anymore: strange Sundays, write-off Mondays, and positively depressed (due to seratonin depletion and fatigue) Tuesdays. Ecstasy, after awhile, is a drug of diminishing returns — the longer you take it, the less enjoyable it becomes and the worse the hangover. GHB is a low-toxicity drug (it is not detectable in urine only four hours after ingestion), and I was told that as long as I didn't mix it with any other drugs, including alcohol, it *had* no aftereffects. This proved true: I had no hangover the next day; all that happened was I fell into an incredibly deep sleep once I went to bed after my night out. This GHB had been nice to take, too — only ten dollars for a tiny vial of clear, almost tasteless liquid that I poured into a five-hundred-milliliter bottle of water and sipped throughout the night. But, above all, GHB felt wonderful. No big bang, just a strong, yet subtle high. An extreme openness that crept up. Like being nicely drunk, but much better. It was tactile, sexy, pleasantly dizzy, and conversation-inducing.

After becoming better acquainted with GHB, which, in low doses gives you a recreational high by both storing and increasing levels of emotion-affecting neurotransmitter dopamine (as one anonymous neuropharmacologist on drugs archive Lycaeum.com puts it, "it plugs up the drain *and* turns on the faucet"), I learned that if I overstepped my limit even slightly — and, with GHB, "slightly" can mean just an extra drop — I could fall, unrousable, into a deep sleep on the spot. Not surprising, given that in higher doses GHB's true function as a sedative emerges (high levels of stored dopamine can put you to sleep).

This fact alone makes GHB an unsuitable substance to take in an environment such as a club. But the real danger of GHB as a club drug is that, when mixed with other substances, even small amounts of alcohol, GHB can have life-threatening effects. As most people taking GHB at places like the Firestone were using it as a replacement for keep-you-up-all-night Ecstasy, many found it too subtle and not energizing enough. They would therefore mix it with cocaine, alcohol, acid, or even Ecstasy itself, creating cocktails that would turn gamma-hydroxy butyrate from lamb into leveler. The biggest problem caused by mixing GHB with other things is that it can cause extreme respiratory depression, because, in addition to affecting emotions, dopamine also affects breathing. So, even on its own, the drug can slow down breathing; when mixed with substances such as alcohol (which also increases dopamine levels, and thus affects respiration as well), breathing slows down even more, perhaps resulting in respiratory arrest, which can sometimes lead to coma or even death. "Respiratory arrest — that became the big trouble," says Eli Tobias, who was a bartender at Firestone. "I think there were many cases."

America, notably the State of Florida, had already been experiencing certain widely reported problems with a sedative called Rohypnol — a drug similar to, but much stronger than, Valium. Clubbers and ravers called Rohypnol "Roofies"; the six o'clock news called it "the date-rape drug." The tasteless, easily dissolved knockout pill was apparently being used, by men (often in college hangouts and country-western bars), to drug unsuspecting women (a dose would be slipped into their drinks) and then take sexual advantage of them. Rohypnol can have an amnesiac effect, so many of these women would be clueless as to what had actually happened to them. The mainstream American media brewed hysteria over Rohypnol: women were repeatedly warned not to accept drinks from strangers, not to leave their drinks unattended, to beware of men leaning close to them and their beverages in bars.

Roofies soon found their way into the Firestone. "Roofies weren't really a problem in our scene at first — it was happening more at frat parties and bars and stuff. But Roofies got to us soon enough," says AK1200. "Orlando's club scene became *the*

Roofie place. People would buy strips of ten [pills] for twenty-five dollars. People liked Roofies, coz, sorta like GHB, they made them feel turned on. Like, real drunk. Roofies make you wanna fuck. Only with Roofies, the next morning you get kinda freaked out because you can't remember a thing: nothing. And so you don't remember if you consented, you don't remember if you were raped. It's not something you want to do with somebody you just met."

"Lots of people did them recreationally, yeah. But I know firsthand that at the Firestone, some men were trying to secretly slip things into girls' drinks," says Tobias. "Some people tried to pay off us bartenders so that we would help 'em spike the drinks they were buying girls. Someone once even dosed me with a Roof at Firestone. I was behind the bar, someone offered me one shot — within minutes I felt like I had drunk twenty shots. Almost got into one of them ambulances myself."

"It was almost as if the Firestone was turning into the Edge," says Orlando house DJ Andy Hughes. "Every weekend, there would be about two ambulances at the club's door, mainly because of GHB — maybe Roofies, too. John Marsa made sure there was a very tight security around the club and ambulances on call because so many people would pass out — which was responsible of him. But to the city and police — well, they just saw ambulances. Ambulances at club doors don't look good." And these ones looked particularly bad. "The Firestone is right downtown, near all the important churches in Orlando, including the one the mayor goes to," explains DJ Remark. "All the strung-out people outside, walking the streets tweaking at 9 A.M.? And ambulances? When all the churchgoers were going to church? Bad news."

◆

While the police, the state government, and the city government were moving in on Orlando's club scene in 1997, a different kind of movement was underway in the music-industry towers of New York and Los Angeles. By the mid-nineties, Seattle grunge had lost Kurt Cobain, and the grunge-led "alternative revolution" was petering out, corporatized to the extent that *alternative* was now a word no American kid would use without attaching a sneer or a roll of the eyes to it. A new "revolution" was needed. Discophobic major labels had overlooked rave in the early nineties. They now had little place else to look for the next big thing, but they didn't know how to sell the zillion different subgenres of house and techno on their own, without an umbrella. All those classifications were too confusing. So classifications were erased, and the suits of Music USA called their decade-late revolution "electronica." Major labels started putting together paint-by-numbers electronica compilations that placed techno with drum & bass, house with trip-hop, party breaks with ambient. Essentially, they grabbed at many different-colored threads and tried to fashion them into one monochrome rope.

Some within America's rave and house scenes (mainly those with money invested) were glad that the industry was finally paying attention. But to many in Ameri-rave, the electronica thing and the press interest and the new MTV shows that came with it felt downright insulting. If you look at street-end music culture and the music industry/press as being a couple that at some point has to get into bed together in order to make big babies, then this was a situation of a lover alone in bed who's been begging for attention. After ten years of romancing others (including old flames), that lonely lover's partner strolls nonchalantly into the bedroom and says, "Ok, let's do it now."

The stars first pushed in electronica were big, established names from the UK, artists who incorporated dance into a "rockin'" live show that even the most staunch Pearl Jam fan could understand: the Chemical Brothers, Underworld, the Prodigy. Later, American artists who could successfully copy these bands' stage/studio formulas, like Vegas's Crystal Method or Orlando's Rabbit in the Moon, became electronica heavies, too.

But there were problems in the packaging of electronica from the start, problems that made this "revolution" seem inauthentic — uneducated, even. The music industry had tried to transform a dance culture into a rock culture, pushing a live-ism that has never been more than a tiny part of the club/rave dancescape. At certain points, it felt like the nucleus of nineties dance, the DJ, had been all but forgotten. Another complication, small in comparison but significant nonetheless, arose from the fact that, by the time the industry had trained the spotlight on electronica, rave and house culture were pan-American phenomena. There was no root place, no convenient historical bedrock that this "genre" could be identified with. Eighties Chicago and Detroit were old stories; by the mid-nineties, they were no longer completely representative, partly due to their gayness and their Blackness. And Europe was too foreign.

In the fall and winter of 1997, American mainstream music publications and style mags, like the men's magazine *Details*, were looking at vibrant electronica (rave) cities through "scene reports" and features. If electronica did not have its own Seattle yet, then there was clearly a push to go out and find one. In the August *Rolling Stone*, the noisemaking "Hot Issue" in which "new" trends and sounds are introduced, Orlando received an eight-page tribute. It was billed by journalist John Weir as the home of America's "Hot Sound" ("electronica!"), and this was buttressed by a sidebar that efficiently explained dance genres from disco to techno (which, weirdly, RS proclaims as a genre of British origin).

The *Rolling Stone* feature, which claimed that Orlando "is not a druggie scene," reenergized the city's already superenergized dancescape. Kids were thrilled that their town had been chosen as the seat of contemporary dance culture in America. The week the glowing RS feature came out, the clubs were more packed and chemicled-up than ever. The feature was such a smash success that the local papers wrote their own articles about it. "It was a euphoric time," says Bevin O'Neil. "We were living in a city described as 'magical,' all the country knew about it, and it had more to do with the Firestone than with Disney. We had it. It was ours. We were electronica central!"

One month after the *Rolling Stone* piece, Orlando mayor Glenda Hood — "Mayor Mom" — set up the Rave Review Task Force and put together an ordinance that the kids on the scene, and even newspapers, called the "Anti-Rave Bill." The main targets were clubs like the Firestone and Ultra Violet, which served liquor until 3 A.M. and then, after-hours, became "juice bars." The ordinance deemed that no establishment could serve liquor past 2 A.m. and all establishments had to close at three — no exceptions. After-hours licenses, even for one-off parties on New Year's Eve, became unobtainable in Orlando. Mayor Hood stationed police officers at every street corner from Thursday night to Sunday night. Then she went on TV, smiled her best smile, and said, just like Nancy Reagan, "This is a war on drugs."

The Firestone's John Marsa was inflamed. He had just installed an expensive new bar in his club, and he had Sasha, John Digweed, and DJ Keoki billed for gigs that he would now have to cancel ("Book a DJ who charges thousands to come play for two hours!?"). Those that kept patronizing the Firestone still arrived, as usual, at 1 A.M., too proud to go out at 11 P.M. like the tourists. Marsa's club soon began emptying. Kids who had moved to Orlando for the scene moved elsewhere. Drugs were increasingly harder to find. The after-hours crowd gave up. They stopped going out, and they waited.

Marsa wrapped himself in the American flag and the Fifth Amendment. He got political. Surrounding himself with a gaggle of lawyers and professional lobbyists, he headed for City Hall with a mission: he would get an amendment to the Anti-

Rave Bill. "Our city had become *Footloose*," says O'Neil, referring to the 1984 teen flick in which Kevin Bacon rallies the youth of an oppressively religious southern town where dancing and "the Devil's music" are illegal. "And John Marsa was gonna be fuckin' Kevin Bacon, man! A true American freedom fighter! A man of his country!" But, unlike what happened in *Footloose*, or in the San Francisco rave scene, where people really did pull together in time of crisis, the Orlando scene gave Marsa only lukewarm support. "He was abandoned," maintains O'Neil. "People were suspicious. His patrons were too stupid to understand what he was doing, and his partners at the club didn't want him to rock the boat."

The boat was already being rocked aplenty. Two weeks before the Anti-Rave Bill was passed, O'Neil — generally known around Orlando as "John Marsa's adopted son" — was hauled out of his own festival, a massive electronica event he orchestrated with two partners called Zen Festival. "There were eighteen thousand people there," he says. "I got arrested for possession of amphetamine." O'Neil insists the amphetamine was a plant: "The mayor and the cops put together a nice plan to get me."

"But Bevin's press was bad all over," says AK1200. "Because the night Bevin was arrested for drugs at Zen, another boy died from drugs — a teenager, in a hotel room five miles out, after the Zen Festival. The media staked out Bevin's house, trying to get him to comment. He had to [bar] himself in. Couldn't get out his door."

It is possible that the lack of support Marsa experienced while fighting antirave legislation was brought on by a general death fatigue among Orlando punters, notably members of the old Firestone crowd, who may have started feeling that their scene was more trouble than it was worth. "I think for many, the pain was starting to outweigh the pleasure," says DJ Andy Hughes. "Maybe some people in the scene even thought what the state and the mayor were doing was a good idea."

It's hard to imagine what else the mayor could have done. Glenda Hood, obviously snuggled up in bed with Disney, was acutely aware that the Disney Corporation basically owned Orlando. And that, according to Disney, the city was supposed to be a beacon of family values and family fun. Hood was getting heat from Disney, from the PTA, from the church, from the media, but she couldn't tell the clubs to clean up their acts because she'd already done that and it hadn't worked. She couldn't set the watchdog-of-society press on the issue because the story had already been thoroughly covered, and it had just made the kids want to go to these parties and clubs even more. Drug education was already being dispensed in Orlando high schools. What was the mayor to do? Plaster the Firestone with parental-advisory stickers?

Marsa was determined to win his "freedom fight," though. At one point, when his battle for an amendment seemed all but lost, he even hired David Wasserman — an attorney who had built his career defending strippers and titty-bar operators — and set out to sue the city on the grounds that Orlando was disallowing "freedom of expression" by imposing curfews on clubs. Lawyer Wasserman told the *Orlando Sentinel*, "these are not just some local guys spinning records." But the argument was too abstract. This lawsuit was asking a judge to declare the bill unconstitutional. There were drugs and drug deaths in the picture. No one had time for the DJ-as-artist issue. Marsa then began a letter-writing campaign to Florida broadsheets, claiming that the bill was a "health hazard": he reasoned that kids would keep on doing drugs, but in more clandestine and less safe environments; he claimed that the Anti-Rave Bill was a badly placed Band Aid solution that "would do more harm than good." His arguments fell on deaf ears.

◆

The Orlando antirave legislation sent the remains of both the breaks scene and the prog scene outside city limits. One of the greatest ironies of the situation was that many Firestone patrons began nightlifing on Disney territory. In 1997 Disney had just completed its multi-million-dollar Downtown Disney "club strip," which included discos and a large House of Blues venue, only a couple of miles out of Orlando. Disney — legally its own "city" — was not affected by the new curfew and drinking laws. Many of Orlando's best prog DJs, like Kimball Collins and Dave Canalte, and promoters, like Stace Bass, took jobs there. "To make a long story short," says Bevin O'Neil (who is still employed at the Firestone — it has survived), "Orlando's real downtown closed, lost all its power, and Disney's fake downtown opened and did double business." In 1998, Marsa was still fighting city hall, lobbying for a 5 A.M. closing time.

The breaks scene fared better due to what Eli Tobias, the former Firestone bartender, calls "a stroke of good luck." After the antirave legislation passed, the owner of close-to-bankrupt redneck "bottle club" just outside Orlando city limits changed his Saturday-night policy from Lynyrd Skynyrd to breaks; he'd twigged to the fact that there were many breaks kids and breaks DJs and no breaks clubs. There are only two clubs with bottle licenses in central Florida — a bottle license allows the patrons to bring their own drinks to an establishment (BYOB) but does not permit that establishment to sell liquor. With no standard liquor license and the right to stay open all night, this redneck club, soon retitled Cyberzone, constituted a useful loophole. Tobias was hired as Cyberzone's "artistic director." He instituted a break-dancing competition — complete with an annual championship match — which remains one of the area's better-attended weekly events, drawing two thousand patrons every Saturday. The lineups for people waiting to get into Cyberzone usually circle the club; young Whites, Blacks, and Latinos tote six-packs of beer. Drug use, says Tobias, is down substantially. "It was meant to be," he says. "Funky breaks and Orlando were meant to go together. It just *had* to work out."

In 1998, break dancing underwent something of a European and American revival. Break dancing was featured in videos by Madonna, Janet Jackson, and Run-DMC (the smash "It's Like That," remixed by American Jason Nevins). New York break-dancing posses like the Rock Steady Crew have been resuscitated and are touring endlessly. In the UK, a funky-fun breakbeat style called bit beat, one that many in Orlando feel is a clean rip-off of funky breaks, has crashed onto the charts, led by Brighton label Skint and DJ/producer Fatboy Slim. West coast funky breakers the Crystal Method have found some success in mainstream America, mainly through film soundtracks.

"Suddenly, the things so many people in Orlando thought were 'kid's stuff' are getting really important," says DJ Icey, who is now signed to label ffrr. Since the Edge, Icey has refused to DJ in Orlando, possibly embittered by the failure of his signature club and the poor reputation funky breaks has in his hometown. "But with the kids, he's still the king of this city," says AK1200. "I guess it's a title he doesn't want anymore. I think Icey's just disappointed by the whole Orlando thing. There was a point where we all felt we could be a really important city. I mean, for something other than mouse ears."

6 THE GAY CIRCUIT
Sex, Drugs, Hot Bodies, and Partying in the Era of AIDS

> A circuit party gives us the chance to escape the pressures of our day-to-day existence and to enter the altered world where man-to-man sex is not only accepted, but is celebrated. . . . When the circuit comes to town, that town becomes an instant gay ghetto full of hot men who are behaving as queer as they care to be.
>
> — *Circuit Noize*

This book is mainly about American rave; in particular I've explored the wide range of forms rave culture took on after it was planted in various centers across North America. But, while writing, I began to feel that I couldn't ignore another kind of all-night dance party that goes on almost every weekend in cities throughout the us and Canada — parties celebrating a culture that has infiltrated the continent far more extensively than rave ever did.

The events that make up the gay male "circuit," a string of huge one-off or annual dances, have, every so often, been called "gay raves."And, indeed, the circuit may on the surface seem to be a phenomenon very close to rave. Like American rave, the circuit is a mainly White society bound together by a series of late-night events that came to prominence in 1991–92. Like rave, the circuit is chock-full of promoters, everchanging venues, favorite DJS, drugs like Ecstasy and GHB, thumping repetitive music, publications, webs of intricate Internet communications, and punters who will travel long distances to attend a party. And, like ravers, circuit boys say they go to the parties for the feeling of unity they get while dancing surrounded by thousands of others who are there for the same reason. They say that drugs help them get to where they want to be on a party night. They assert that naysayers "just don't understand" that circuit parties are about more than escapist light shows, steep ticket prices, subversive behavior, and elaborate dress codes — that parties are a way of life and a major source of identity for the circuit's regular patrons.

It's hard to imagine that all these similarities are coincidental; still, the two dance cultures run along separate arteries that have not merged. The history of rave can easily be tracked as a musical history: what happened to disco when it became house; what happened to house when it became acid house and techno; what happened to acid house and techno when they could no longer be contained in nightclubs and had to move into field, warehouse, auditorium. The history of the circuit is only half musical: it traces what happened to the disco that became hi-NRG instead of house; but, more definingly, it follows what happened to disco culture when it met something distinctly nonmusical. When, in gay life, the "disco era" became the "AIDS era." When people started dying, and the gay community began searching for ways of raising money. One way, as it turned out, was special dance parties; already a tradition in the gay night scene, they would undergo a makeover in the 1990s and reemerge as fundraisers.

◆

Like rave culture, circuit culture has some roots in the seventies, was born in the eighties, but came to full fruition in the nineties.

But, because it doesn't find any sort of starting point in the British rave boom of the late eighties — as the subjects of most chapters in this book do — I'll have to start this history quite a bit earlier. I'll have to delve into some of the stuff I described in the first chapter — stuff that was going on in the New York clubland that many people interviewed for this chapter describe as "pre-AIDS."

House and all of its musical babies have made up the dominant — or at least the most written-about — dance culture of the past decade. So the New York discos of the late 1970s that fed directly into house — the Loft, Paradise Garage — have become the most revered, the most exulted for their historical importance. These places were certainly a crucial part of the gay experience in New York's disco era, but now, as they enjoy a retrospective popularity, they have been reconceived: the tutti-frutti pushcart of 1970s Big Apple disco has become one bearing only, say, two fruits.

Places like the Garage, were, within their era, known as "mixed" clubs. They were blind to class. While mostly gay, they also had some straight patrons, and women were admitted. These establishments attracted a mainly Black and Latino crowd, although some Whites went along as well. They were often described in the gay community as soul or R&B clubs rather than just discos.

On the other side of the gay spectrum were places like the Flamingo or the Twelfth Floor, fabulous private gay discos with louche decor and exclusive, terribly expensive, yearly memberships. Patrons of these nighteries also frequented less-glitzy after-hours clubs like the Anvil and 12 West, where beautiful, gym-pumped, masculine White males who lived in the gay ghetto of Chelsea met others like themselves. This side of the New York gay spectrum soon built a mega disco called the Saint. "If you want a really obvious picture," says former Saint party-organizer Rod Rockerick, aged sixty-eight, "the Garage was mostly Black and music-oriented — like, all that mattered to [Garage patrons] was their R&B-disco-soul music — and the Saint was White, right from the start. People who went to the Saint didn't like the Garage. Some joked that [Garage investor] Mel Cherren only got interested in the place because he had a thing for Black boys. The Saint was more status 'n sex 'n drugs-oriented than the Garage — which isn't to say that to some gay men it wasn't as spiritual a place." The Saint is where the story of the circuit begins.

◆

The Saint was built at the tail end of the golden gay disco age, in 1980. A last-wave disco. The kind that could not have existed before disco became rich with the commercialization of the late 1970s and had begun fragmenting into specialized niches catering to this sort or that sort of patron. The Saint chose a very specific type of "new gay man" as its client — not only affluent, but also the sort adhering to the burgeoning "cult of masculinity" that was visible at places like the Flamingo, the Anvil, and 12 West; White men who shunned the queeny "sissyness," the flamboyance, the drag shows that to them may have symbolized what being gay was all about *before* gay liberation.

"In the late seventies something happened," says Kerry Jaggers a handsome blonde Texas DJ and lighting designer who was a Saint regular. "Suddenly some bars and clubs were full of men who looked like *men*. Like, masculine men who just happened to like other men. Gay men who had [appropriated] the straight idea of 'macho,' who *hated* the notion that being gay was all about being a sissy queen." Men who wore ripped T-shirts, work boots, and Levi's 501s to go clubbing. Men who would take off their T-shirts on a midnight dance floor and loop them through the waistbands of their jeans, exposing pecs that could only be achieving by toiling all day in a granite pit — or working out at a high-end Chelsea gym. "'Gay clones.' That's what they became

known as," says Jaggers. "Many of them were professionals —
gay lawyers, accountants . . . they were who the Saint was made
for, a crowd that ten years prior literally *did not exist.* They became the Saint prototype."

They — these so-called clones — were also artists, designers,
writers, producers, entrepreneurs, activists, jet-setters, and often
"hot boys" who just looked gorgeous. They were the meat and
potatoes of what was increasingly being called the "gay A-list":
typically, well-heeled, social-pages people who indulged in luxurious urban nightlife during the colder months and settled in
beach houses on the exclusive, primarily gay resorts of Fire Island
for the summer.

This crowd was a tough nut to crack, and so the Saint was
designed to be one of the most, if not *the* most, aesthetically
impressive gay nightclubs that New York City had ever seen. For
six million dollars, the old Fillmore East concert venue on Second Avenue and 6th Street, capacity seven thousand patrons, was
transformed into the flash, shining king of all macho haunts.
The music at the Saint was also flashy and shiny; Euro and electronic disco, a sound soon increasingly titled hi-NRG (first,
Giorgio Moroder and Boney M; later, Miguel Brown's "So Many
Men, So Little Time" and the entire oeuvres of Frankie Goes to
Hollywood and Hazell Dean), the "trashy dance" sound the club
has since become known as having helped develop. The Saint
instituted a strictly men-only and members-only policy (members could bring in nonmembers only if they called ahead and
had their guests approved). The club did not provide for a cheap
night out, but, almost instantly, its membership list was impen-
etrably full.

◆

Everyone who went to the opening of the Saint in 1980 said it
felt like the dawning of a new era, a new world, even — a world
too big to fit into any one city, including New York. The creator

and owner of the Saint, Bruce Mailman, who also owned the city's most famed gay bathhouse, the Saint Marks Baths, said he wanted the Saint to be a place where all time, space, and limitations evaporated, an area where lights and immense sound became space and time itself. There were no columns or harsh corners anywhere in the club, and the dance floor, which could accommodate almost three thousand, was perfectly round. Round, and covered by what was then the largest planetarium dome on the East Coast, which rose from one side of the dance floor. Behind the skin of the dome was a balcony, which was one of the club's major attractions. It could only be reached via two spiral staircases. "That was the sex area," says Jaggers. "There would be two thousand people there having orgiastic sex openly, guiltlessly, every hour of the night. It was beautiful. It defied description."

At about four o'clock every morning, the DJ — the Saint featured such resident DJS as Warren Gluck, Michael Firemen, Roy Thode, and Robbie Leslie — would cut off the hi-NRG music. Then the "sleaze music," the sultry, pretty morning music (like the Police's "Every Breath You Take,"" or Bonnie Tyler's "Total Eclipse of the Heart") would start. At this point, the cosmos would be projected onto the skin of the dome — people say it felt like you were dancing in outer space, that you couldn't even feel your feet on the floor. Of course, the drugs helped: the MDA, the THC, the PCP, the LSD, the poppers, the Quaaludes, the Xanax, the Ketamine, the coke, and the MDMA — MDMA being, of course, Ecstasy, the then-legal drug that was just debuting on the Saint scene and rapidly becoming popular. With these pharmaceutical friends, everything belonging to real life just melted away until it was time for you to leave the club, early the next afternoon.

◆

The Saint was always at its most sexy and decadent on the night of an official bash. The club put on two very special events every year. The White Party and the Black Party. At the White Party, everybody wore white (it was Easter), and the club was decorated fancifully. At the Black party (an event that actually preceded the Saint — it had first taken place at the Flamingo), the theme was S&M/leather, live hardcore sex shows were featured, and there was an air of masculinity even more intense than usual. Parties like these, and similar events at West Coast clubs like the Probe superdisco in LA, or the one-offs thrown by San Francisco's Boys in the Sandbox, gave rise to an elite coterie whose members would fly back and forth between New York and California, enmeshed in what was becoming known as the "gay circuit." These traveling partygoers, who would fill their weekends with trips to gay bathhouses and nightclubs, dinner parties, and private cocktails dos before the big bashes, could be called the first "circuit boys." Holding down prestige jobs during the week, they would flit off to glamorous destinations to indulge in nonstop sex, drugs, and dancing on weekends.

Kerry Jaggers remembers the White and Black Parties at the Saint well: "The parties were like a meeting of the tribes. All of the tribes part of a bigger tribe, a tribe gaining confidence and unity. I remember thinking at the last [White Party] I went to that things had finally changed for gay men . . . . I was watching a buncha guys who were scared for a large part of their lives — scared of their sexuality, of being found out, scared of each other. Those people [were] blossom[ing] and bloom[ing] and it was magical . . . . It was, like we had *won*! We were partying in the name of our freedom. And the future looked brighter than ever."

✦

In early 1982, the acronym AIDS had not yet been invented. Many in the gay community called it "gay cancer," as the mysterious illness was still generally thought to be the fixed property of homosexual men. In the medical community, it was referred to as GRID, Gay-Related Immune Deficiency. In New York City, where, in March of 1982, over half of the country's three hundred reported GRID cases were situated, one oft-used name for the illness was "the Saint disease." At the time, it seemed, almost exclusively, to strike the type of New York gay man who went to that club: those who had indulged in weekends of drugs and multiple sex partners, who had long held membership at both the Saint and the Saint Marks Baths, who had traveled the circuit and shared beach houses with friends and lovers on Fire Island. The "A-list" gays.

By the summer of 1982, a palpable fear was building in gay New York. "People still didn't know it was a sexually transmitted disease. Even doctors didn't really know — all they could say was, 'Yup, this disease is killing you,'" says Jaggers, who was diagnosed with HIV in 1990. "It was commonly thought that this *thing* — this horrible set of symptoms killing people — could have come from some envionment[al] cause. Was it poppers? Was it bad air in the [Saint] club? Could you get it off the toilet seats? From mixing drugs? From MDA? From Ecstasy?" Some researchers at the Center for Disease Control in Atlanta were still seriously questioning whether a bad batch of poppers or another popular club drug could have triggered this disease that had struck so many gay nightclubbers. "Everything was so unclear. People were beginning to be afraid. I mean, people were dying, and all we had to go on was the odd rumor or announcement. Some people stopped going to the Saint, and places like that altogether."

It was a couple of years before the question mark of GRID became the understood reality of AIDS, a sexually transmitted disease, and then the Saint's decline accelerated rapidly. The Saint's Bruce Mailman, was one of the first New York gay business owners to take an active interest in the fight against AIDS, raising money and once or twice donating the club for fundraisers.

"But, by 1984, people were dropping like flies," says Jaggers. "Some blamed Bruce Mailman, because people went to the Saint or the Saint Marks Baths to have sex. He was looked down upon as killing people's friends, and the club became very controversial."

◆

In his definitive history of the AIDS epidemic, *And the Band Played On*, Randy Shilts explains how the government of New York City, the hardest-hit metropolis in the Western world in terms of AIDS cases, was criminally negligent in dealing with the realities of the disease. Mayor Ed Koch turned a blind eye throughout the first half of the eighties. There were no funds, no specific programs, very little public education. The New York City administration seemed intent on ignoring the mounting crisis, on leaving it to the badly stricken gay community to worry about.

New York City's approach to AIDS mirrored that of the Reagan administration: as if this messy little problem that affected so many gay men would just go away if they ignored it long enough. Even when straight hysteria erupted over the disease in 1983, fueled by some irresponsible newspaper and journal reports claiming that AIDS could be spread through "casual contact" (experts knew by then that it couldn't), the Reagan administration remained unwilling to allocate more than a pathetic fraction of the funds needed to fight the disease — all the while smiling and assuring the public that AIDS was its "number-one health priority."

It is within this atmosphere of governmental whitewash and community anxiety that the first grassroots AIDS group, the Gay Men's Health Crisis, was born. The GMHC set out to raise both money for, and awareness of, AIDS. In the early 1980s, private donations were not forthcoming, so the GMHC decided to try fundraisers.

The first was a flop. It consisted of a card table planted on a Fire Island beach on Labour Day, 1981. Beneath a banner reading "Give to Gay Cancer," the GMHCers sat and waited. They thought they would collect thousands, as Labor Day weekend was always a big party on Fire Island. It was a balmy day, and the island was indeed swamped with gay fun seekers, but at the end of it all the GMHC's take was a mere $124.

People came round for the second fundraiser, which was scheduled for April 8, 1982. It took the form of a party at the Paradise Garage, the club Shilts describes in *And the Band Played On* as "one of the less popular discos" — which to the Saint/Fire Island party crowd that attended the benefit, it *was*. Tickets for the event, called Showers, were available in gay shops and bathhouses across Manhattan. The pavement outside the Garage was lined with revelers before the club even opened for the night. The GMHC had cracked the fundraising code, raising over fifty thousand dollars in one night.

When GMHC chairman Paul Popham took the stage to address the crowd, the words he spoke would foreshadow the rallying cry of the 1990s circuit scene, the scene this pioneering GMHC party was helping to create: "It may be that an equal measure of fear and hope has brought us together, but the great thing is, we *are* together." A couple of months later, the GMHC threw its first annual Morning Party, an open-air DJ dance event on the beaches of Fire Island. The Morning Party attracted hundreds more than even the Paradise Garage fundraiser had. People came from all over America especially to attend the event. The Morning Party — the double meaning of its name signifying both the hope and the despair of the gay community in the era of AIDS — could be described as the first truly modern circuit party. Partying for a cause was now the newest way to dance the night away.

◆

The Saint finally closed in 1987, at which point two-thirds of all American AIDS cases were to be found in the New York City area. The club died a gradual death as the phrase "AIDS is killing the Saint" chipped away at its reputation. The Paradise Garage closed the same year, but the Garage's culture, by then the culture of house music, continued to flourish, even in the AIDS-addled New York of the late eighties, through clubs like the Shelter, Better Days, the World and the infamous after-hours spot, the Sound Factory, which opened in 1989.

The A-list and clone side of clubland New York — that is to say the muscled, cruising, Saint side — didn't seem as if it was going to weather the AIDS storm quite as well. Some members of that crowd were in denial, frequenting bathhouses and back-rooms as if the disease didn't exist. But many just stopped going out. They were petrified. "There was a noticeable difference for a couple of years," says Jaggers; "even Fire Island in the summers — always a bustle — seemed a bit dead."

Yet the success of a handful of fundraisers like the annual GMHC Morning Party would soon create a new weekend option for the Saint crowd. By the early nineties, the guilt and confusion over AIDS had gelled into an understood, and terrible, but almost banal truth in New York's gay community. The Saint annex of clubland had mobilized again, forming the decade's fundraising circuit: a linking of parties not unlike the original Saint-event-to-Probe-event circuit, only generated by a charitable cause and boasting greater travel opportunities. These parties, which always came complete with a cluster of before and after parties, soon became a major leisure attraction for the more affluent, "masculine-type" gay male.

Circuit parties started drawing not hundreds, but thousands, sometimes tens of thousands. Lure DJs like Junior Vasquez and Victor Calderone, or "pure circuit" names like DJ Buc, Joe D'Espinosa, and Susan Morabito, were brought in. By 1992, it was not unusual to hear of gay men traveling across North

America to attend these NRG/house events (circuit-sound music is best represented by the fast Italo-NRG house of Living Joy's trashy 1994 track "Dreamer," or Junior Vasquez's quintessential Madonna remixes, usually topped off by Saint-style "sleaze music" in the later morning). The events took place in ballrooms, sports arenas, stadiums, armories, amusement parks, beaches, ski lodges, convention centers. Fresh travel agencies began cropping up in big American and Canadian cities that catered to this newly conscious gay jet-setter — a type lovingly referred to as the "circuit queen." The circuit queen did not spend regular dollars: he used what the media had begun called "gay dollars." A new industry had been launched and, along with it, a new lifestyle. The spirit of the Saint had been resurrected and was on an airplane bound for New Orleans, Montreal, Miami, Palm Springs. The circuit was spreading across America with amazing efficiency. Some would say — actually some circuit critics *have* said — it was spreading as fast as a disease.

◆

I couldn't even begin to name every circuit party in existence at present. There were over fifty circuit weekends in North America in 1998. There were also events in the popular circuit locales of Australia and New Zealand, as well as within the burgeoning scenes of Europe. The circuit has become so vast that it has started to subdivide out of sheer necessity. Now, there are major circuit parties, like the White Party in Miami, the *other* White Party in Palm Springs, Miami's Winter party, Hotlanta, the Black and Blue in Montreal, the Hellball in San Francisco, Mardi Gras parties in New Orleans, and Gay Pride parties in New York City. Most are fundraisers; some — like the Black Party, now thrown by a group called the Saint-at-Large, or the White Party in Palm Springs (no relation to the original Saint White Party) — are not, but they are still considered part of the circuit. In addition to the majors, there are regional parties: smaller events held in less alluring locales like the Red Party in Columbus, Ohio. Finally, there are off-circuit events — such as Miami's Phoenix Rising parties — that take place between the major parties or latch onto big-party weekends. Many of these off-circuit parties happen in minicircuit clubs like Miami's Salvation or New York's Splash — clubs set up to appeal to the local and the out-of-town circuit boy.

The world of the circuit seems wondrous to the outsider, and to many insiders it is even more wondrous. It's an exclusive, super male environment quite like the Saint created, only a zillion times bigger. It is a place where well-heeled or well-pumped gay men party guiltlessly — these days not "in the name of freedom" but usually for another good cause: AIDS. It is a world where everybody can afford a plane ticket to Miami or Palm Springs, not to mention a hotel room and loads of chemical party favors. Where circuit queens can hold down nice jobs and still jet off anywhere they like and carouse on weekends as though Monday would never come.

It is a clone world where all the men are fantastically, ideally gorgeous. All are tanned. All are muscled. All have designer jeans or sunglasses or underwear or expensive gym memberships. It is sexy and glamorous like no club culture has been since disco. Like, when was the last time you went to a poolside cocktail dance at a resort hotel where every room was filled with cool party people and then headed off to an all-night party where there was a $150-dollar cover charge and ingested all the drugs you wanted while hobnobbing with the rich and beautiful? It's like a Herb Ritts-directed video! A fancy liquor commercial! And everybody in it seems happy, fulfilled, free, and full of life. The circuit supports the fight against a terrible disease, but it all seems as far removed from a terrible disease as anyone could imagine. "Going to [circuit] parties," circuit sage and scene chronicler Alan Brown once wrote, "is much more about self-preservation than self-destruction . . . . I'm not quite ready for my appointment with obliteration, thank you. I simply can't go without that Prada bag that I've always wanted . . . ."

But, over and above the money and the glamor, circuit punters will tell you that the best thing about their larger-than-life society is the sense of well-being and unity they experience during a fabulous weekend or excellent party. "I love the circuit. I have found in the circuit a home and a place where I don't feel weird, more than I've found [it] anywhere else in the gay community," says Steven Baird, a corporate lawyer who is also the chairman of the Winter Party in Miami. "The circuit is full of fascinating, gorgeous people. The [circuit] is also a testament to our economic power, our corporate power, and our power as a community. We are fighting against AIDS, fighting for gay issues, and we are doing it together. And that feels wonderful."

◆

The Black and Blue party in Montreal is the largest circuit event in North America. After the annual nonprofit AIDS fundraising event had succeeded in luring over twelve thousand people in 1996, it turned itself into the Black and Blue Festival. By 1998, it was featuring over twenty-five different events, all surrounding the climactic official party with DJ Victor Calderone. Eighteen thousand people were in attendance at the 1998 Black and Blue: the event had come a long way from the small, private fundraising dance held in an auction house that was the first Black and Blue, in 1991.

Montreal is an exemplar for circuit advocates like Steven Baird, who claims that the circuit is a good way for the gay community to make a name for itself in mainstream, corporate society. Robert Vezina, head of the Bad Boy Club Montreal, which organizes the Black and Blue, appears to have a love affair going with Montreal City Hall. Like many circuit promoters, Vezina would not be considered your average clubworld type: he has a well-established background in corporate PR, as well as an honors degree from McGill University, and his respected family resides in historic Outremont, an affluent, largely Francophone, Montreal municipality.

An impressive man. But that's not the only reason the city likes him. Montreal, the largest, most cosmopolitan city in the province of Quebec, has been in the throws of a deep recession since the late eighties, and tourism has suffered. Yet the city is always miraculously revived the week of the Black and Blue: hotels are packed and streets are filled with shoppers and people in search of a good restaurant. Most have come to town for the big event. On average, more than 70 percent of the Black and Blue crowd is from out of town. Since its inception, the party has generated over sixty-five million dollars in tourism spinoffs for Montreal. "No city can ignore that," says Vezina. "It gives power to the gay community."

It's this kind of power — corporate power — that the circuit loves showing off. In terms of undergroundism, it's the exact opposite of rave culture. In circuitland, the more corporate and commercial you are, the more legitimate. One look at the 1998 Black and Blue flyer confirms this: the names of sponsors like Molson Breweries, Air Canada, and the Greater Montreal Tourism Bureau are featured as prominently as the names of the DJs that were slated to play. Like that of hip-hop, another culture with roots in social oppression, the circuit's self-image seems to be bolstered by waving money around. You've got to show that you have it, "and if you have it," remarks Baird, "you can have it all. And if you don't, some parties are just out of reach."

The most expensive circuit event in 1998 is the White Party in Miami at $150 a head. The Black and Blue, however, is seen as a reasonably priced event: entry to the main Black and Blue party in 1998 was sixty dollars Canadian at the door. A gold VIP pass, which permitted entry into all twenty-five events, was three hundred dollars. It can be argued that this kind of spending can only benefit the AIDS cause, since the Black and Blue is, after all, a fundraiser. But, given the event's huge production costs, the Bad Boy Club Montreal has, since 1991, donated only $650,000 to AIDS charities. It's a lot, yes. But place that next to the sixty-five *million* that the Montreal tourism industry has raked in and things come into perspective: in the world of the circuit, leisure has superseded charity. Fundraising is now far from being the circuit's raison d'être.

Almost fifteen thousand people attended the Black and Blue in 1997. Montreal's famed Olympic Stadium was done up in silver and blue. The view of the dance floor from the mezzanine was astounding; spread below was a sea of skin and lasers, a breathtaking apocalypse of people and mega-high-end technology. On that balcony I met Jason, an immaculately tanned man in his mid-thirties, wearing black army boots and blue hot pants — attired in black and blue, as the party flyer had recommended.

Jason told me that he was a "total, 100 percent circuit queen," and that he traveled to at least ten different circuit events every year. I was looking for people to interview for an article I was writing about the circuit, and so Jason and I found a corner to chat in, in front of some heavy sound curtains, away from the sweaty masses. We both got a bit of a jolt when we realized that some people just behind those sound curtains were engaged in activities that would get them thrown out of the party if they were discovered by the Black and Blue's newly instituted "sex police." "Now this — right here — all of this, this kind of love," Jason said, pointing to the moving sound curtains and then to the ecstatic dance floor, "this is liberation. So remember it."

Jason, a lawyer by profession, explained that he worked out every single day. He was proud to say that, unlike many circuit queens, he didn't use steroids to get that essential "circuit look." He loved taking drugs at big circuit parties, especially Ketamine, but when he returned to work at his sleek New York law firm after circuit weekends, he was always professional. His colleagues did not know he was gay. He said he was "hard to spot" when his top wasn't off and his shaved chest and Navy style tattoos weren't out there for all to see.

"Work, gym, circuit, sex — if I'm lucky," he told me that night, standing under a banner advertising Wet International lubricant, explaining how he divided his time. "I guess that is my lifestyle." I looked around at the Black and Blue revelers, all shirtless, all with their body hair shaved or waxed off to promote a "youthful look," all tanned, all tattooed, all with crewcuts just like Jason's, all clad in jeans or little shorts, all on amazing drugs. "Is that what all these people do, too?" I asked. Responded Jason: "Lots of them. That's the circuit. It's like a religious ritual. You work for money, you gym for body; you make the most of money and body at the party. It's worth it. The circuit is the ultimate escape. You can forget all your troubles, all the shit of day-in-day-out just evaporates Everybody doing the same thing — it's, like, wow! The feeling is amazingly strong, like, really emancipating."

There is no question that getting high and dancing with thousands of other people a lot like you can feel liberating and that escape can be productive, creative, and fun. I wasn't too sure about the other stuff, though — especially, "work, gym, circuit, sex — if I'm lucky." That didn't sound too liberating to me. Nor have attitudes like this sounded liberating to many gay men, who, in recent years, have begun mounting a pretty vocal backlash against the developing culture of these parties. "What the circuit has done in a big way in recent years," says Montreal journalist and gay-activist Matthew Hays, who has written for gay magazines like the *Advocate* and has long tracked parties like the Black and Blue, "is that it has set up a kind of cultural cage. The thing I find most surprising, when I go to a circuit party is the astonishing sameness from a community that has developed through bucking conformity. I find it odd that we have now created our own codes of conformity, codes often borrowed from the straight world. The gym body, the 'healthy,' athletic tan, the clothing, the haircuts, the macho tattoo: the cult of masculinity that began in the 1970s has gone haywire. I do find it all a bit disturbing and discouraging."

Hays, who describes himself as "a bit queeny, not exactly muscular," finds the modern circuit frighteningly elitist, even "fascistic": "Because if you don't have the body, you are not 'in.' You can't really participate — nobody will look at you, not when everybody else has that stuff." To people like Hays, circuit promoters have simply said "If you don't like it, then just stay away." Which is a good point. "Yes," says Hays, "but that's becoming harder. Our biggest problem is that the circuit boy has become the most desirable thing, the thing many gays, on or off the circuit, want to look like, to follow. It's in all the magazines, the gay newspapers; it's become the overriding aesthetic. The circuit has an influence far beyond the confines of the parties now, and it's breeding a widespread body dictatorship."

It could be argued that this kind of "healthy body" worship is an aesthetic response to AIDS. Pump yourself up, look healthy, and then people will be less inclined to think you have HIV or ever could have it. It's interesting to note that a lot of people go straight to the gym when they find out they have HIV. "It's almost a knee-jerk response," remarks Hays. "Even if they don't have it, people don't want to look like they have it, don't want to look skinny, so they go to the opposite extreme." Strength over sickliness. Celebration over pain and mourning.

"I think," continues Hays, "it was [gay author] Brad Fraser who said that the circuit is like a 'time pill.' You go to these parties and it's all pleasurable excess: there are these bodies all around you, you are taking mind-altering substances, you look great, you forget, your emphasis shifts from the present-day reality, and boom! Before you know it, you are back at the disco, back to the pre-AIDS era."

Hays is not the only circuit critic who has watched the astonishing growth and influence of the culture and proposed that a lot of this partying phenomenon is riding on nostalgia for a time before AIDS. A time when you didn't have to worry about wearing a rubber. You didn't have to witness your friends dying. You didn't have to fear becoming sick yourself. Many circuit boys are too young to even remember such an era, but they might dream about it anyway. "In recent years, there has been a resurgence in the rentals of pre-AIDS gay porn, — porn without rubbers," says Hays. "There is a kind of AIDS fatigue floating around the gay community now; people are sick of thinking about it, so this kind of nostalgia is very potent. Which I totally understand. But that's not to say it isn't very dangerous."

◆

Dangerous because of unsafe sex. One of the craziest ironies of the AIDS fundraising circuit has been that it is such an unconducive environment for the promotion of safe sex — even though many circuit parties *are* AIDS fundraisers, and even though there *is* always a banner or two or a booth where free condoms are handed out or "safe fucking" videos are screened. Because, quite honestly, when you are raving on drugs, feeling superfly, surrounded by walking porno covers, are you really going to pay much attention to a *booth*? When you're in an altered state, are you really aware of your actions at all, and do you want to be made aware? In the heat of the moment and the wow of a high, in the sweet folds of "pre-AIDS nostalgia," would all those advance warnings be enough to hold you back from having sex without protection?

Most drug agencies and AIDS organizations would say "No." And even the staunchest circuit queens will admit that the circuit and recreational drugs are inseparable, that it's harder to think safe when you're high. Steven Baird thinks that some drugs are more dangerous in respect to safe sex than others.

"Lots of people, I'd say most, can't ejaculate or can't even get it up on Ecstasy, and so I don't think Ecstasy, a drug which so many circuit-trashing [critics] have demonized, is any problem at all. It will just get a buncha guys hugging and dancing — not having sex. Ketamine, very popular on the circuit, is another drug that almost acts as a chemical condom . . . the majority would find it extremely hard to penetrate on ketamine, as erections are not easy on it. So, tell me this: when you have two thousand guys on ketamine or E and they can't penetrate, how, just how are they going to give each other this disease?"

Of course, not everyone is on E or ketamine. All kinds of drugs are apparent on the circuit, as they are in rave. A drug like Ecstasy can be just the starting point for the hardcore fun seeker's long chemical voyage. And, not unlike the way it was in the American rave scene, by 1995, two other recreational drugs had become very popular on the circuit: GHB, considered a sexual stimulant by some; and methamphetamine, otherwise known as crystal meth. The former became a "big problem" as people would "fall out" on it (as described in the Orlando chapter of this book). Crystal meth, however, became what some saw as a safe-sex calamity.

Crystal is a long, strong, impulsive drug. And it won't leave you flaccid. All sorts of urban tales abound about men who've had sex for eight hours straight on it, or men who masturbated all day and all night until their penises bled — stories of extreme reflex. "It's cheap, it can last days if you take enough, and it is . . . yes . . . it is dangerous" says Baird, who also allows that the use of crystal may have reached epidemic proportions on the circuit, an opinion shared by substance-abuse specialists in gay ghettos like West Hollywood or the Castro in San Francisco. "I know this from conversations with friends, from my own experience," says Baird. "Meth will lead people who would never, never have unsafe sex to have it. People used to say this about coke, but meth is much more sneaky because it has this way of insidiously affecting people's behavior. Meth goes in through your brain's back door; you forget you're on something. It gives the illusion of, like, fantastic everything, you lose your conscience, and, yeah . . . . There's been a lot more crystal on the circuit lately. A few years ago, I never even knew what crystal was. Now it's everywhere."

"Crystal is the worst. The worst," says West Virginian DJ Buc, one of the top circuit DJS. "I can tell you, I was a junkie, I used to shoot two and a half grams a day — you get hooked on it so easily. I don't know about 'epidemic.' I don't think most of these circuit guys are junkies — they just do it a lot . . . . And, at a circuit weekend, you can be constantly partying for two, three days, very easily and of course that alone lets down your inhibitions. I know what it's like to be up for two days. Your mind plays tricks on you."

In 1996, for the first time in about ten years, the number of gay men with AIDS was up in cities like Miami and LA. In one 1996 study of Miami's South Beach gay population conducted by respected AIDS researcher Dr. William Darrow, 75 percent of all men questioned said they had participated in condomless anal sex within the previous year. The question of whether the circuit was actually assisting in the spread of AIDS became a source of heated debate. Baird, like most other circuit lovers, says that the circuit should not be blamed for statistic like these or for instigating "bad behavior" among its proponents. This is the same type of argument that issued from parts of the gay ghetto in the eighties, at the inception of the AIDS epidemic; don't shoot the messenger. If it wasn't happening on the circuit, it would be happening anyway. "In nightclubs, or whatever," says Baird. And DJ Buc agrees: "The circuit is wonderful. Drugs are dangerous. And if queens weren't doing them on the circuit, they'd just do them somewhere else. That's a fact."

But critics — like writer Michelangelo Signorile and playwright and former GMHC bigwig Larry Kramer, two radical gay activists with very big soapboxes — countered this, saying that the circuit *was* an unhealthy environment. They pointed to extreme recreational drug use; they also pointed to circuit queens giving themselves skin cancer by overusing suntanning beds and charring their insides with illegal, often dangerous steroids to get "the look." These people were displaying a total disregard for health at the expense of beauty (a practice clearly not exclusive to the circuit, but one these critics believed was too deeply ensconced in the circuit value system). Signorile and Kramer then went on to caution against yet another disturbing practice: something called "barebacking," or "bareback riding," or "going raw." This is the practice of intentionally having sex without a condom. People on the circuit say this activity should not be identified with their scene; activists like Signorile and Kramer believe it is inextricably linked to the culture that has developed out of these circuit parties.

◆

Palm Springs is an oasis in the southern California desert, a lush, hot place, nestled beneath the monumentally high, snow capped San Jacinto Mountains. It is one of America's most upscale resort towns, and, like so many other warm resort destinations in America, Palm Springs harbors a strange idiosyncrasy: it has a transient gay population and a humongous senior-citizen population that either ignore, or are simply unaware of, each other. Located about two and a half hours out of Los Angeles, Palm Springs is also a second home to many LA moneybags: film executives, movie stars, sports pros. It's an immaculately greened-up and well-watered cluster of nouveau-riche tennis clubs, restaurants offering golden agers early-bird dinner specials, and gay spas and underwear shops. Approaching Palm Springs by car, you'll see nothing but miles of scraggly desert, and then suddenly a paradise of intense leisure will appear — a blooming, manicured townsite with trees fastidiously trimmed to look any shape but tree shape.

John (not his real name), a thirty-three-year-old buyer for a chain of stores, had his first true bareback experience in Palm Springs. It was during the 1997 celebrations surrounding one of the most exalted parties on the circuit: the Palm Springs White Party (no relation to the Miami White Party or the original Saint White Party).

Says John, "OK, here's the scenario. My initiation. It was the night of the main event, and I was totally partied out. There were all kinds of before parties — a fabulous pool party and stuff — and I had used up all my energy at those doing K and E and coke. I'm no crystal queen, I wouldn't touch that. Anyway, I decided to miss the main party. I felt gross and ugly and was into getting an earlyish night. I go to so many circuit parties that I didn't really care about missing this one, even if it was the *faaaabulous* White Party. I was staying at the most oddball hotel, not the Wyndham or the Hyatt or the Marriott Courtyard, where everyone wants to stay, or even at one of those cute mom 'n pop inns, but at this real trashy place. I actually forget what it was called. Anyway, it had this huge, sleazy casino in the lobby. Part of the casino only had a tentlike canvas as a roof — real cheapstown — and I thought it was funny, so I went in there to blow off some time and have a drink. All my friends had gone off to the party, anyway."

"The casino was kind of depressing," John continues. "You had to pay a dollar to play a hand of blackjack, and the place was stuffed with slot machines and Mexicans and trailer-park trash with these cups of coins, just, like, losing *everything*. Anyway, I saw this guy who was definitely a circuit boy — buff, tattoo, two loop earrings — at one of these machines, and I sat next to him. He said that he never went to main events, because he liked the small parties better, because they were more private feeling, like exclusive. And, after a couple of minutes of talking, we realized that we had grown up in small towns right next to each other and even knew a couple of the same people from our childhoods. It was so cool. Like, those kinds of connections are why I love the circuit.

"So," says John, "to make a long story short, we were up in my room in no time, and this guy was pulling out a water bottle with GHB [in it], casually asking me if I was neg or poz [HIV positive or negative]. I was, like, 'Yeah, I'm neg,' and he was, like, 'Me too, I swear.' So I thought, 'cool' — it's always a relief hearing that. But then he suggested something that was so racy, I couldn't believe it. He said he was into doing it 'raw' — you know, bareback riding; and that he was a top — you know, he liked to be the one [penetrating]. He also said he was really turned on by the fact that I was a bareback virgin."

"Of course I *knew* about barebacking, everyone on the circuit knows about it. We are a very Internet-literate community, and the bareback stuff is all over AOL, especially with poz groups, but I never thought of doing it. But this night I guess my inhibitions were down from the E and K hangover I was on — oh, and the coke, and plus the GHB we were drinking . . . you could say I wasn't all there. And as soon as we started kissing, the connection we had *did* seem very close, and very super . . . all that stuff about growing up near each other, like, having the same accent and knowing some of the same people in our childhood. I just thought, 'Yes. This is right. I want to feel more of this connection and a condom is a barrier.' A condom is, like, reality and I was in what I like to call total 'circuit-weekend perfection,' the part of the weekend when you are so stuck in it all that you have no feeling of time or real[ity] — just beautiful pleasure. You're not thinking, just doing. So I did it."

John says that "once you bareback, you don't go back." He is still seronegative, and he now has a network of friends in various circuit cities who are into doing it raw, too. "They are all neg," he says, "but once in awhile I go out on a limb with someone I don't know." John says he enjoys this kind of sexual roulette because the danger is exciting, "and the feeling is amazing, for sure."

But he adds "Look, don't get me wrong. I don't have a death wish or anything. I look at people who are on the new combination [AIDS] drugs, the protease inhibitors, and their T-cell counts are back to normal. They are totally healthy. And some of them, because they can now have guilt-free sex without a condom — they have nothing to lose, they have HIV already — their sex lives are better than ever. So, if I get it and I can live healthy for, like, twenty years, have great sex, and maybe start running into problems when I'm almost a senior? Honestly, that's kinda OK. Part of me doesn't want to be a pathetic old queen still hanging around anyway."

◆

Barebacking, an extremely marginal practice, is the most radical manifestation of the kind of carefree, youthcentric, live-for-now-ism that has come to characterize the circuit. Only a few men on the circuit would call themselves all-out barebackers. Most of the ones I interviewed used words like "disgusting," "suicidal,'" and "incomprehensible" to describe the raw practice. Yet the psychological motivations of barebacking culture do seem incredibly close to those of the circuit. The thinking behind both cultures is virtually identical. It's the celebration of *now*. The pursuit of pleasure. The wish to be closer to other gay men, physically *or* spiritually. A determination to stop living under the shadow of AIDS.

Like the circuit itself, barebacking raises incredibly complex issues, and the deeper you go, the more complex they become. People like John, looking for other neg guys to have "better sex" with are actually the less extreme sector of the barebacking populace. For extremists, there are Internet sites like xtremesex.com, where "poz-hungry men into bareback sex" can meet. "Poz-hungry" men are those hungry for "the gift" of HIV-positive semen. And HIV-positive semen is the ticket to bareback land, where it's all great guiltless sex — or, as John puts it, there's "nothing to lose." You "have HIV already."

"This attitude has come since the new AIDS drugs, the protease inhibitors," says Matthew Hays. "They have created a false sense of security. There are a lot of gay people probably thinking that the AIDS crisis is over, that getting it is no longer fatal."

In 1997, a University of California at San Francisco study reported that protease inhibitors, the drugs that can dramatically prolong the lives of some patients with HIV and AIDS, have a failure rate as high as 53 percent, when not taken faithfully. "But people don't know this," continues Hays. "A lot of the [ignorance] has to do with the patchwork, piecemeal way the protease inhibitors have been covered in the mainstream media: like, 'A Cure for AIDS!' The media has been obsessed with showing these people who have started, miraculously, feeling better. Their viral count is zero. They are suddenly working out again and getting muscles, or they are back on their job. And that's great. But I think there has been a lot of focus on that and less on the fact that inhibitors are a Band-Aid, not a cure, and no one knows how long they will last. They are [also] very hard on your system. Not to mention that many researchers are worried that the combination of unsafe sex and the drugs could lead to a super-AIDS strain that is resistant to the treatment. Anyway, all that aside, the drugs don't even work for everyone."

In 1997, Robert Vezina told me that he believed "the phenomenon of barebacking" was linked not only to the new hope that has come from these drugs, but also to the socioeconomic issues surrounding them, issues that smack of the circuit's infatuation with material wealth. "The new combination drugs for AIDS, the [protease] inhibitors, are working incredibly well, which is amazing," he said. "But the drugs are expensive, and, even with all kinds of AIDS programs, not everyone can afford them or has the health insurance to cover that kind of expensive medication. The people who can are the same people who can have houses on Fire Island, can fly to Palm Springs for the weekend. I think fucking without a condom has become a status symbol. Like, 'I can afford these drugs if I need to.'"

Vezina now says he has changed his mind. Hays thinks that the theory Vezina put forward in 1997 and discounts today makes sense. "I wouldn't snub that idea," he says. "It is true that if you were rich you could have far better health insurance to take care of you. There are thirty-five million people in the US who are not insured, and if they had to go on some catastrophic drug program they'd have to be bankrupt first before they could get anything. I think Robert [Vezina] might be afraid of being associated with that theory because he's a circuit promoter. He doesn't want to put blame on the same moneyed class he is trying to attract."

◆

In 1997, Michelangelo Signorile's *Life Outside*, an examination of aspects of gay life inside and outside the circuit, hit the bookstores. Since the late eighties, Signorile had been one of the most controversial men in gay intellectual politics; he'd earned his reputation through his journalistic practice of pitilessly "outing" celebrities in print without their permission. Music-industry baron David Geffen, one of Signorile's victims, called Signorile "a terrorist" in a 1989 *Advocate* interview: "An angry, hostile, jealous guy who has his nose pressed up against the window at the party that he imagines is going on but that he hasn't been asked to." Almost a decade later, men on the circuit would be saying exactly the same type of thing.

Referred to occasionally as the "McCarthy of the Left," Signorile was already disliked on the circuit before *Life Outside*. After his stint of outing celebs, he made a new name for himself by writing columns and articles that critically pried open circuit culture, pieces that appeared in publications as diverse as *Out* magazine and the *New York Times*. But with *Life Outside*,

Signorile officially became the circuit's own persona-non-grata scribe; the despised Truman Capote of the circuit; the person who knew about it all, had an opinion about it, and wasn't afraid to put it in print. Circuit boys called him "antisex," "right wing," and, as Steven Baird put it to me, "antigay."

Or, more precisely, anti-urban-gay-lifestyle. Signorile supports gay marriage and gay monogamy. He exalts gays who move out of the fast life of ghettos/scenes like Chelsea in New York City and the Castro in San Francisco. He thinks the circuit (to him the apex of gay ghetto culture) is creating an influential class of what he calls "Stepford homos" — muscled robots "frighteningly conditioned" and "hypnotized" to "mold themselves in the image of the circuit ideal" and ignore issues like drug abuse, safe sex, and gay-rights activism.

Visiting Palm Springs for the White Party, the flammable Signorile was outraged by a number of things, and he lays them out in *Life Outside*. One of these is the fact that a Marriott hotel was being used as an official party hotel. Marriott being a company owned by "devout Mormons." Marriott being a company that donates 15 percent of its annual net profits to what Signorile calls the "viciously homophobic Mormon Church." A church that "exerts its muscle [by] teaming up with the religious right and the Catholic Church to roll back gay rights across America."

"From the Mormon's perspective," Signorile sputters, "why not indeed let the fags blow off some steam, let the fags take their drugs, let the fags have their unsafe sex? Why not let the fags go on infecting themselves with a deadly disease? Why not let them believe protease inhibitors are a cure? Let them perpetuate their rigid physical ideals and bolster their oppressive rules of masculinity. And let them believe that in doing all this they are achieving true liberation. All of that, after all, will keep them contained . . . . ."

This, of course, is all hypothetical: the Mormons were unlikely to have known anything about the gay "cult of masculinity" or about the orgies and drug fests Signorile witnessed at the White Party. But Signorile's completely nonhypothetical indignation at the circuit scene is well represented in the preceding passage. One particular thing inevitably got his goat. He couldn't fathom how gay health groups could link their names to these parties. How could AIDS groups like, say, the GMHC, the most respected AIDS charity in America, dare to throw this type of event, dare to raise money off the very things they were battling against? Wasn't that tantamount to the Cancer Society taking money from the tobacco industry?

Needless to say, Signorile's literary furor did not sit well with the passengers on the circuit-party trains and with many others as well. The battle lines were drawn, with many noted gay intellectuals, journalists, doctors, and social workers on Signorile's side. As I said earlier, Michelangelo Signorile has one of the biggest soapboxes in the gay intellectual world. He was going to stir things up further, it was clear, and he had support. The circuit defended itself in Internet discussions and in magazine articles appearing in publications such as *Circuit Noize*, as well as in local gay magazines, notably those coming out of big circuit destinations like Miami Beach. The defenders argued that the circuit was an economic force that made the gay man important in the straight world. That events like the GMHC Morning Party raised millions for AIDS causes. That the circuit created a loving, secure haven for its initiates. That it was a much-needed balm in an otherwise harsh world. A form of identity of which circuiters were proud. And (echoing what rave-scene advocates have always countered in their battles against moralizers), that dancing on drugs is as old as Adam: it's liberating, goddamn it, and that Signorile . . . well, he must be jealous.

Of course, jealousy must be the root of his problem, they said. "The most vicious and vindictive 'reporting' on the circuit has originated in our own community, with the famous and formerly useful Michelangelo Signorile leading the charge," wrote

Steven Baird in a 1999 issue of the Florida gay mag *Miamigo*. ". . . I believe that the root of much of this internal gay criticism of circuit parties lies in the rejection felt by some who don't think they are pretty or hip enough to fit in at a circuit party, a feeling of rejection that is in large part internally derived. These people, almost in spite of themselves, literally hate collections of beautiful male bodies having a good time."

✦

Like the rave scene, the circuit didn't originate as a place of excess. Escape, maybe, but not excess. But, like the rave scene, after a couple of years the circuit *became* a place of excess. I'm not tut-tutting the trajectory: I'm just calling it inevitable. Drugs that, with a single dose, once helped you escape, have now become familiar to your body. You need to take two pills. Three pills. Four pills, the content of a vial, half a blotter, and a few bumps. Whereas you once found a party fun, now you need a whole weekend of parties, even a long weekend packed with before-before-parties and after-after-parties. The bar that stands between you and escape rises and rises. Before you know it, you have reached excess. You are on a cocktail of chemicals, dancing at yet another party, spending twice as much money as you did at similar events a couple of years before, wondering why things don't feel as good as they used to. So you take another pill, stay up another night, hoping to get that feeling back again. That feeling could be the orgasmic high of your first-ever E tablet. Or, to stretch things a little further, in the case of the circuit, that feeling could be the sexual honeymoon of the pre-AIDS 1970s.

Like every other rave scene in the world, the American rave scene was, for the most part, fractured by excess. Usually, at some point or another, the police would crack down, then the fragmentation process would quickly follow. Yet the circuit won't suffer the same fate anytime soon. There is too much municipal and corporate money tied to circuit events, and any police force would think twice before shutting down an AIDS fundraiser, given the political reverberations. So, for the circuit, at least initially, the shut-downs — which are just as inevitable as the excess that triggers them — will come from the inside. From a moral police force within the gay scene powered by people like Signorile.

In 1998, this sort of campaign — lead by none other than Signorile — had already begun. Articles were being published everywhere. In the mainstream media, the sentiments were uniform. "Circuit parties are like piling up wood for a bonfire right in the center of what has been a huge, devastating forest fire that looked like it was just starting to die down," Dr. Judy Wasserheit, director of the sexually transmitted disease division of the Center for Disease Control and Prevention told the *Los Angeles Times* in October of 1997. "If you were a virus, you couldn't think of a more wonderful place to spread."

No one could close down the whole circuit, the fifty-plus major weekends spanning America, but enough pen power could be mustered to topple one symbolic party. So the target became the most revered of all circuit events, the most seminal of all parties, one of the most anticipated events of the year: the GMHC Morning Party. In 1996, a man was evacuated from the remote Fire Island beach site of the Morning Party by helicopter after falling into a drug-related coma. This was major ammo; so was the fact that the GMHC had actually organized this party rather than just hooking up with a promoter who had decided to do a fundraiser, as most other circuit sponsors tended to do.

There were countless editorials on the topic in the twelve months that followed the 1996 Morning Party helicopter incident, the fiercest being Signorile's in the *New York Times*, published days before the 1997 Morning Party: "There is something hypocritical about groups that try to encourage healthful lifestyles but that benefit from parties where drugs have become a problem . . . . When [the] Gay Men's Health Crisis and other

AIDS groups put their names on invitations and on the glossy ads for such parties that abound in gay publications, they help promote a cultural phenomenon that undercuts the very important work they are doing. There are better ways to raise money, and AIDS groups, GMHC included, surely know about them."

For several years prior to this, the GMHC had been offering drug-and-alcohol-abuse seminars on Fire Island during Morning Party week. All the group could do in 1997 was increase police visibility and keep its fingers crossed. There were so many cops at the 1997 Morning Party that some revelers said it felt like a police state. Thankfully, no one died that year, and doctors in the party's first-aid tent reported treating nothing more dramatic than cuts, scrapes, and sand in contact lenses. In 1998, though, there was a Morning Party-related death: a Bronxville, New York, man died of a drug overdose — GHB was implicated — in the predawn hours before the party. The GMHC could not be held responsible, even though the Bronxville man had most probably been headed for the organization's event. The celebration went on. A big pink birthday cake was planted in the middle of the Fire Island beach site, proudly announcing the party's "Sweet Sixteen." Almost half a million dollars was raised for the Gay Men's Health Crisis.

But the GMHC was already staggering under the year's barrage of criticism, and another Morning Party-related death was not something it could sweep under the carpet. In December of 1998, the organization sent out a news release with the headline "GMHC Will Not Hold Fire Island Morning Party in 1999." "Regrettably," it read "over the past few years the Morning Party has become associated with alarming levels of recreational drug use, despite GMHC's many attempts to discourage drug-taking at the event . . . . White it is painful for us to end this Fire Island tradition, it is more painful that the Morning Party's reputation for drugs undermines GMHC's year-round efforts to educate people about substance abuse and how it relates to HIV infection."

◆

The backlash against the backlash has now become an integral part of the circuit experience. Ending the Morning Party, the circuit party that had raised more money for AIDS initiatives than almost any other of its kind was controversial. "If you have to close one down," says Steven Baird, "why not shut down a nonfundraising party? Why not, like, the Saint-at-Large's Black Party? That party has a *backroom* [for anonymous sexual encounters], for God's sake! Why shut down a party that is raising so much money?"

In January of 1999, a month after the GMHC sent out its press release indicating the termination of the Morning Party, Signorile told the *New York Times* that it would be "more difficult for other [AIDS] groups — in Miami, in Chicago, in Los Angeles — to continue to host these circuit parties now that GMHC, the leading sponsor, has pulled away, because these groups around the country are also receiving this kind of pressure from within the gay community." Many money-starved representatives of AIDS organizations, however, have hesitated to fulfill this prediction, maintaining that they must take money from wherever they can get it. After all, with the "new hope" instilled by the protease inhibitors in recent years, private donations have dropped significantly.

The circuit is still growing by leaps and bounds, and it seems likely to keep doing so for the time being, with or without the AIDS-fundraising engine. This trend is embodied by promoter Jeffrey Sanker, who throws circuit events, including the Palm Springs White Party, for his own profit. Sanker now throws about thirty-five different circuit parties in various cities every year.

"Oh, it's growing," says DJ Buc. "When I'm DJing at a circuit party, I watch these thousands of people on the dance floor and sometimes I can't believe it. Like, I think this is something indescribable — the size, the beauty. But can it last? Sometimes parties feel too good to be true, and I think a lot of men on the circuit are afraid that one day, something will stop the parties. But maybe that's the point. Like dancing on the edge. As a DJ, I can tell you it's something that will always go on, in one form or another, and if people fall off — well, honey, there will just be a new group of people to replace them."

Bibliography

Aaron, Charles. "Drums and Wires" [electronica]. *Spin* Sept. 1996.

Altman, D. *The Homosexualization of America.* Boston: Beacon, 1985.

Anonymous Article on Toronto's Exodus club. *Punter* 1(1992).

Armstrong, Steven. "Pretend That We're Cred" [superclubs]. *The Face* Aug. 1996.

Baird, Steven K. "Bitter Table for One? A Defense of Circuit Parties." *Miamigo* Feb. 1999.

Beadle, Jeremy J. *Will Pop Eat Itself?: Pop Music in the Soundbite Era.* London: Faber, 1993.

Berger, P.L. *Face Up to Modernity.* London: Penguin, 1977.

Bones, Frankie. The Bones Report. *Streetsound.* Nov./Dec. 1990, May 1991, Aug. 1991, Jan. 1992, Nov. 1993, Dec./Jan. 1993, Aug. 1995.

Braunstein, Peter. "The Last Days of Gay Disco." *Village Voice,* 24 June 1998.

Broughton, Frank. "Chicago, Still Rockin' down the House," *i-D* Apr. 1995.

Bruni, Frank. "Drugs Taint an Annual Round of Gay Revels." *New York Times* 8 Sept. 1998.

Buckley, Jonathan, and Mark Ellingham, eds. *Rock: The Rough Guide.* London: Rough Guides-Penguin, 1996.

Budd, Lawrence. "Shooting from the Lip" [profile of Firestone lawyer David Wasserman]. *Orlando Weekly* 9 Oct. 1997.

Champion, Sarah. "Fear and Loathing in Wisconsin." Redhead, *Club Cultures.*

———. "Kids in America: From Rockers to Ravers." *i-D* Sept. 1995.

———. "Techno Prisoners" [Drop Bass Network]. *Melody Maker* 28 May 1994.

Champion, Sarah, ed. *Disco Biscuits.* London: Sceptre, 1997.

———. *Disco 2000.* London: Sceptre, 1998.

Cheeseman, Phil. "The History of House." *DJ* 22 Apr. 1993.

Chronopoulos, Sandy. "Kings of the Jungle" [Toronto jungle]. *Tribe* 36.

Cocoran, Cate C. "Dancing on the New Edge" [Toon Town and smart drugs]. *San Francisco Bay Guardian* 9 Oct. 1991.

Collin, Matthew. "Party On!" [British sound systems]. *i-D* Feb. 1991.

Collin, Matthew, and John Godfrey. *Altered State: The Story of Ecstasy Culture and Acid House.* London: Serpent's Tail, 1997.

Collin, Matthew, and Mark Heley. "Summer of Love." *Energy Issue.* Spec. issue of *i-D* [month?] (1989).

Cook, Samanatha, Tim Perry, and Greg Ward. *USA: The Rough Guide.* London: Rough Guides-Penguin, 1998.

Cosgrove, Stuart. "Seventh City Techno" [Detroit techno]. *The Face* May 1988.

Curtius, May and Michael Ybarra. "Gay Party Tour: More Harm than Good?" [sex and drugs on the circuit]. *Los Angeles Times* 13 Oct. 1997.

Curvin, Laura, and Darren Ressler. "Orlando: The Next Magical Musical Kingdom?" *Mixmag* Dec. 1996.

Daas, Ram. *The Only Dance There Is.* New York: Aronson, 1976.

DaSilva, John. "The Whole World Is a Disco." *DJ* June 1992.

Dunlap, David W. "As Disco Faces Razing, Gay Alumni Share Memories" [Saint club retrospective]. *New York Times* 20 Aug. 1995.

Eckes, Kurt. Interview. With Beverly May. *Transcendance* fall 1996.

E.G., Mark. Drop Bass Network profile. *Eternity* Sept. 1998.

Flaherty, David H., and Frank E. Manning, eds. *The Beaver Bites Back?: American Popular Culture in Canada.* McGill-Queen's UP, 1993.

Fleming, Jonathan. *What Kind of House Party Is This? The History of a Music Revolution.* Slough, Eng.: MIY, 1995.

Frith, Simon. *Performing Rites: On the Value of Popular Music.* Cambridge: Harvard UP, 1996.

———. "The Suburban Sensibility in British Rock and Pop." *Visions of Suburbia.* Ed. Roger Silverstone. London: Routledge, 1997.

Garratt, Sheryl. "Sample and Hold" [Chicago house]. *The Face* Sept. 1986.

——. "The We Generation" [orbital rave]. *The Face* Dec. 1989.

Garret, Laurie, and Jesse Mangalman. "A Deadly Epidemic of Denial" [gay unprotected sex]. *Newsday* 30 May 1995.

Gendin, Steven. "They Shoot Bare Backers, Don't They?" *poz* Feb. 1999.

Godfrey, John, Ed. *A Decade of i-Deas: The i-D Encyclopaedia of the '80s.* London: Penguin, 1990.

Haden-Guest, Anthony. *The Last Party: Studio 54, Disco, and the Culture of the Night.* New York: Morrow, 1997.

Harpin, Lee. "Jungle Massive." *The Face* Aug. 1994.

——. "Rumble in Toronto's Jungle." *i-D* Apr. 1995.

Harris, Daniel. *The Rise and Fall of Gay Culture.* New York: Hyperion, 1997.

Harrison, Melissa, ed. *High Society: The Real Voices of Club Culture.* London: Piatkus, 1998.

Harvey, Steven. "Behind the Groove" [New York djs in the early 1980s]. *Collusion* Sept. 1983.

——. "Get That Perfect Beat" [New York disco djs]. *The Face* Oct. 1983.

Haslam, Dave. "dj Culture." Redhead, *Club Cultures.*

Hays, Matthew. "Dancing on Our Ashes" [gay pride]. *Montreal Mirror* 30 June 1994.

Hermes, Will. "Garage Schock" [electronica vs rock]. *Spin* Sept. 1996.

Hill, Dave. "Boystown Nights" [hi-NRG]. *The Face* Sept. 1984.

Hills, Gavin. "Bug-Eyes, Bloodshot and Full of Love" [Berlin's Love Parade rave]. *The Face* Aug. 1994.

——. "Wonderland UK" [drug habits in the uk]. *Face* Jan. 1993.

Holmes, Andrew. Profile of Joey Beltram. *dj* Sept. 1995.

Hughes, Walter. "Feeling Mighty Real: Disco as Discourse and Discipline." *Village Voice Rock and Roll Quarterly* summer 1993.

Jones, Fabio. Uprising. *XLR8R* 16.

Kramer, Larry. "On the Politics of aids Research." *gmti* Feb. 1995.

Lewis, Kevin. "Was This Man the Best *dj* in The World?" [Larry Levan]. *Jockey Slut* Jan 1998.

Marcus, Tony. "Acid Daze" [San Francisco rave]. *The Destination Issue* (1992).

Marsa, John. Editorial [on the Orlando club scene]. *Orlando Business Journal* 11 Apr. 1997.

Massive, Matt. Profile of Even Further. *Massive* 19 Mar. 1998.

McBean, Sharon. "Club Sues Orlando over Rave Shutdown." *Orlando Sentinel* 1 Jan. 1998.

McClelland, Susan. "The Lure of the Body Image" [gay body image]. *Maclean's* 22 Feb. 1999.

McDownell, C. *Dressed to Kill: Sex, Power and Clothes.* London, Hutchison.

McKay, George. *DiY Culture: Party and Protest in Nineties Britain.* London: Verso, 1998.

McReady, John. "Did Depeche Mode Detonate House?" [Detroit techno]. *The Face* Feb. 1989.

Moynihan, Michael, and Didrik Soderlind. *Lords of Chaos: The Bloody Rise of the Satanic Metal Underground.* Los Angeles: Federal House, 1998.

Norris, Chris. "Pop Music Fall Preview" [electronica]. *New York* 8 Sept. 1997.

"100 of the Best Things to Happen This Year." *i-D* Dec. 1987.

"One Nation under a Groove" [a history of acid house]. *Muzik* Mar. 1998.

Owen, Frank. "The Kind of Ecstasy" [Lord Michael and New York rave]. *Village Voice* 1 Apr. 1997.

Owens, Sherri M. "Raves: Is Party Over or Just Relocating? *Orlando Sentinel* 15 Sept. 1995.

Palmer, Tamara. "Coming of Age" [American rave culture.] *Urb* July/Aug. 1998.

Park, Jan Carl. "News from the Saint" [interview with DJ Robbie Leslie]. *Star Dust* Mar. 1983.

Pierce, Kim. "Federal Government Cracks Down on the Use of Ecstasy." *Dallas Morning News* 7 Jan. 1985.

Prince, David J. Profile of Drop Bass Network. *Urb.* Apr. 1996.

Prince, David J., and Kevin Martin. "Welcome to the MPD Rave" [Milwaukee Grave Rave]. *Reactor* 3.

Puccia, Joseph. *The Holy Spirit Dance Club* New York: Liberty, 1988.

"Radical Chic." *i-D* Dec. 1987.

Redhead, Steve, ed. *The Club Cultures Reader.* Oxford, Blackwell, 1997.

Reynolds, Simon. *Energy Flash: A Journey through Rave Music and Dance Culture.* London: Picador, 1998.

———. "Rave Culture: Living Dream or Living Death?" Redhead, *Club Cultures.*

———. Review of Even Further. *Melody Maker* 13 July 1996.

———. "Rrrrr-Rush!" *Melody Maker* June 1992.

——. "Technical Ecstasy." *Wire* Nov. 1992.

Richardson, Lynda. "Study Finds H.I.V. Infection is High for Young Gay Men." *New York Times* 16 Feb. 1999.

Rietveld, Hillegonda. "The House Sound of Chicago." Redhead, *Club Cultures*.

Robins, Cynthia. "The Ecstatic Cybernetic Acid Test" [San Francisco rave]. *San Francisco Examiner Magazine* 16 Feb. 1994.

Romero, Dennis. "Spinning in the Spotlight" [American rave DJs]. *Los Angeles Times* 25 June 1995.

Rose, Cynthia. *Design after Dark: The Story of Dancefloor Style*. London: Thames and Hudson, 1991.

Rose, Tricia. *Black Noise: Rap Music and Black Culture in Contemporary America*. Hanover: UP of New England 1994.

Rotello, Gabriel. *Sexual Ecology: AIDS and the Destiny of Gay Men*. New York: Dutton, 1997.

Rushkoff, Douglas. *Cyberia: Life in the Trenches of Hyperspace*. New York: HarperCollins, 1994.

Rutherford, Paul. "Made in America: The Problem of Mass Culture in Canada." Flaherty and Manning.

Sack, Kevin. "H.I.V. Peril and Rising Drug Use." *New York Times* 29 Jan. 1997.

Salamon, Jeff. "Aces in the Crowd" [electronical]. *Spin* Sept. 1996.

Saunders, Nicholas. *E for Ecstasy*. London: Nicholas Saunders, 1993.

——. *Ecstasy and the Dance Culture*. London: Hicholas Saunders, 1995.

Scarce, Michael. "A Ride on the Wild Side" [barebacking] *POZ*, Feb. 1999.

Schoofs, Mark. "The AIDS Race: Can New Drugs Keep up with the Wily Virus?" *Village Voice* 10 Feb. 1999.

Seiler, Tamara Palmer. "Melting Pot and Mosaic: Images and Realities." *Canada and the United States: Differences That Count*. Ed. David Thomas. Toronto: Broadview, 1993.

Shilts, Randy. *And the Band Played On: Politics, People, and the AIDS Epidemic*. New York: Penguin, 1987.

Signorile, Michelangelo. "Bareback and Restless." *Out*, July 1997.

——. "Beyond the Good Gay/Bad Gay Syndrome." *Newsday* 17 Aug. 1997.

Smith, Andrew. "Safer House" [Ecstasy testing]. *The Face* Oct. 1995.

Smith, Russel. "Starck Raving Madness" [Starck Club]. *Dallas Morning News* 8 Oct. 1985.

Staricco, Paul. "The Underground: Truth or Trend." *XLR8R* 18.

Steven, Colin. Profile of the Toronto jungle scene. *Knowledge* Feb./Mar. 1998.

Stevens, J. *Storming Heaven: LSD and the American Dream.* New York: Grove, 1998.

Strauss, Neil. "All-Night Parties and a Nod to the 60s (Rave On!)." *New York Times* 28 May 1996.

———. "Electronica 101." *Spin* Sept. 1996.

Thomas, Rebecca. *Break, Rattle and Roll* [breakdancing]. *Orlando Sentinel* 17 July 1997.

Thornton, Sarah. *Club Cultures: Music, Media and the Subcultural Capital.* Hanover: Weslyan UP, 1996.

Toffler, Alvin. *The Third Wave.* New York: Bantam, 1981.

Toop, David. *Ocean of Sound: Aether Talk, Ambient Sound and Imaginary Worlds.* London: Serpent's Tail, 1995.

Toop, David, and Paul Rambali. "Hip Hop Won't Stop" [electro]. *The Face* June 1984.

"Vogue's View" [feature on rave fashion]. *Vogue* Dec. 1997.

Weir, John. "Hot Sound" [Profile of Orlando rave and dance music] *Rolling Stone* 21 Aug. 1997.

Welsh, Irvine. *The Acid House.* London: Jonathan Cape, 1994.

Wernick, Andrew. "American Popular Culture in Canada: Trends and Reflections." Flaherty and Manning, *Beaver Bites Back?*

Yardley, Jim. "Gay Charity Event Seen as Sending the Wrong Message." *New York Times* 2 Jan. 1997.